P9-AQQ-828

3 5000 08570 42

DOROTHEA DIX

Other titles in *Historical American Biographies*

Historical American Biographies

DOROTHEA DIX

Crusader for the Mentally Ill

Amy Paulson Herstek

Enslow Publishers, Inc.

40 Industrial Road	PO Box 38
Box 398	Aldershot
Berkeley Heights, NJ 07922	Hants GU12 6BP
USA	UK

http://www.enslow.com

Library of Congress Cataloging-in-Publication Data

Herstek, Amy Paulson
    Dorothea Dix : crusader for the mentally ill / Amy Paulson Herstek.
        p. cm. — (Historical American biographies)
    Includes bibliographical references and index.
    ISBN 0-7660-1258-1
    1. Dix, Dorothea Lynde, 1802–1887—Juvenile literature. 2. Women
social reformers—United States—Biography—Juvenile literature.
3. Mentally ill—Care—United States—History—Juvenile literature.
[1. Dix, Dorothea Lynde, 1802–1887. 2. Reformers. 3. Women—
Biography. 4. Mentally ill—Care—History.] I. Title. II. Series.
    HV28.D6 P38   2001
    362.2'1'092—dc21
    [B]
                                                        00-011478

Printed in the United States of America

10 9 8 7 6 5 4 3 2 1

To Our Readers: We have done our best to make sure all Internet addresses in
this book were active and appropriate when we went to press. However, the
author and the publisher have no control over and assume no liability for the
material available on those Internet sites or on other Web sites they may link to.
Any comments or suggestions can be sent by e-mail to comments@enslow.com or
to the address on the back cover.

Illustration Credits: Enslow Publishers, Inc., pp. 75, 81; Library of
Congress, pp. 6, 23, 29, 40, 44, 47, 49, 56, 62, 70, 73, 88, 89, 94;
National Archives, p. 15; Reproduced from the *Dictionary of American
Portraits*, Published by Dover Publications, Inc., in 1967, pp. 19, 34, 35,
45, 66, 85.

Cover Illustration: Library of Congress (Inset), © Corel Corporation
(Background).

CONTENTS

Dorothea Dix is best remembered for her work as a Civil War nurse, but her most meaningful work was her eloquent appeal on behalf of the mentally ill.

"I Tell What I Have Seen"

In January 1843, Dorothea Lynde Dix's first "memorial," or speech, to the Massachusetts legislature was presented at the statehouse in Boston. Her address was a powerful statement. It drew attention to the plight of the poor, mentally ill inhabitants of prisons and almshouses—what would be called homeless shelters today—throughout the state. Dix had spent two years investigating the ghastly living conditions of the mentally ill. She had been profoundly shocked by what she had seen. Now it was time to share what she had viewed firsthand with the men who had the power to improve the condition of the mentally ill—the Massachusetts state legislators.

"I come to present the strong claims of suffering humanity," Dix wrote:

> I come to place before the Legislature of Massachusetts the condition of the miserable, the desolate, the outcast. I come as the advocate of helpless, forgotten, insane . . . men and women; of beings sunk to a condition from which the most unconcerned would start with real horror.[1]

Throughout her address, Dix cautioned that she was presenting "cold, severe facts." She wanted to assure her audience that she was not overreacting. "If I inflict pain upon you, and move you to horror," she said, "it is to acquaint you with sufferings which you have the power to alleviate, and make you hasten to the relief of the victims of legalized barbarity."[2]

Dix insisted she was only the messenger—"*I tell what I have seen,*" she said.[3] What she had seen was the cruel manner in which the mentally ill were kept. It was not that prison wardens intended to be cruel, Dix explained. They just did not know any better.

For the most part, Dix's assessment was correct. In mid-nineteenth-century America, medical treatment for those suffering from mental illness was virtually nonexistent. Often, if the person's family was wealthy, the ill person was cared for at home—usually kept indoors and out of sight. For the insane poor, however, there was no recourse but to jail them or let them wander aimlessly. Frequently, they were imprisoned with murderers and other felons or they were sent to an almshouse with other poor people. They received no treatment for their illness. They were simply kept out of the public eye.

When Dorothea Dix began her investigation, a process that became an inventory of Massachusetts jails and almshouses, she was shocked and horrified by what she saw. In every prison and almshouse she visited, she saw mentally ill people chained to the wall. Sometimes both their hands and feet were shackled. Some were caged in cells smaller than a horse's stall. Often, they were imprisoned and physically bound merely because they were ill.

A careful inventory of living conditions and the mental state of each individual prisoner is what she presented to the Massachusetts legislature. "Three idiots [a common term of the time for certain mentally ill people]; never removed from one room. . . . One idiot, one insane; most miserable condition," she wrote of two prisons she visited.[4] Many inhabitants were naked, yet lived without heat or proper bedding.

When Dix visited Berkeley, Massachusetts, she came across a townsman and asked if he could give her directions to the almshouse. The man told her the way and added that there were "plenty of insane people and idiots there."

"Well taken care of?" she asked.
"Oh, well enough for such sort of creatures," was the man's reply.
"Any violently insane?" she asked.
"Yes; my sister's son is there, a real tiger. I kept him here at my house awhile, but it was too much trouble to go on; so I carried him there," the man responded.
"Is he comfortably provided for?"
"Well enough."
"Has he decent clothes?"

"Good enough. . . ."

"Food?"

"Good enough; good enough for him."

"One more question," she said, "has he the comfort of a fire?"

"Fire! fire, indeed! what does a crazy man need of fire? A red-hot iron wants fire as much as he!"[5]

Outraged by the man's ignorance, Dix resolutely marched to the asylum, where she dutifully wrote down the scene she saw before her: "These gross exposures are not for the pained sight of one alone . . . all, witness this lowest, foulest, state of miserable humanity."[6]

Dix had gathered information in other ways, too. On a fateful day in 1841, Dix reportedly had been asked to find a suitable woman to teach Sunday school to the female inmates of the Middlesex County Jail in East Cambridge. Without hesitation, she jumped at the chance to do it herself.

Dix began to teach Sunday school to nearly twenty female inmates at the prison. The women had been jailed for offenses ranging from theft and prostitution to simply being poor and homeless.

After class, Dix passed by a cell with a woman in it. Her only "crime," Dix was told by the jailkeeper, was being mentally ill. The woman's cell had no heat, and the woman was not clothed properly. When Dix asked the warden why it was so cold in the cell, he reportedly said—just as the man in Berkeley did—that it was because the insane do not know the difference between heat and cold. Outraged but inspired, Dix soon began what would become her life's most meaningful work: reforming and improving living conditions of the mentally ill.

Dix called on the Massachusetts legislature to "devise a remedy for the evils now attending the unfortunate pauper lunatic and idiot."[7] She concluded: "Gentlemen, I commit to you this sacred cause. Your action upon this subject will affect the present and future condition of hundreds and of thousands."[8] Having seen the atrocities of which she spoke firsthand, Dorothea Dix dedicated the rest of her life to finding a suitable place—a home—for the mentally ill. Her crusade would take her around the world and into predominantly male corridors of power. It would carry her through the American Civil War, and span nearly forty years of her life.

2

OUT OF THE WILDERNESS

Dorothea Lynde Dix was born into unfortunate circumstances and harsh New England winter weather on April 4, 1802, in Hampden, Maine (part of Massachusetts at the time), a frontier town six miles south of Bangor. Dorothea's parents, Joseph and Mary Dix, lived in a one-room cabin. For their first child's birth, Joseph had rented a room at a neighbor's home to provide more comfortable—and warmer—surroundings, a common practice at the time.

The Dix family soon returned home, where Dorothea's father resumed his work as a traveling Methodist minister. He journeyed throughout the New England frontier, attempting to convert the people he met along the way. It was a hard life, but one to which Joseph Dix claimed he felt a religious calling. In reality, it could be said that it was the latest turn in a long downward spiral for the family.

Only one hundred fifty people lived in Hampden. Most of them were as poor as Joseph and Mary Dix, living in small cabins with oilpaper windows and dirt floors. Men cut timber or trapped animals for their fur in winter and tried to farm the rocky New England soil in summer, growing corn, potatoes, and pumpkins. Women cared for the house. In addition to cooking and cleaning, they were responsible for performing the essentials required for running a home: making soap, gardening, spinning flax, knitting, churning butter, making candles, and sewing clothes. Children tended the farm animals, knitted, sewed, gathered firewood, and looked after younger siblings. There was no time for play. If any free time could be found, it was spent in religious activity such as reading the Bible or praying.

The Dix Family

The rough Maine woods were no place for a sensitive man like Joseph Dix. He was born on March 26, 1778, in Worcester, Massachusetts, the third of seven sons born to Dr. Elijah and Dorothy Lynde Dix, and the only one who survived to adulthood. Joseph's father, Dr. Elijah Dix, was an ambitious, self-made man. After completing an apprenticeship at the age of twenty-two, he mastered the art of medicine and set up shop in Worcester, Massachusetts. The industrious Elijah Dix "approached health care like a competitive business," and he quickly prospered.[1] He expanded his business to include a chemical manufacturing plant and made a fortune in shipping and real estate. On October 1, 1771, Elijah Dix, a successful man but a social outsider, married one of Worcester's most attractive young women, Dorothy Lynde. She was considered the "belle of Worcester" and came from one of the most prominent families in town.[2] Dorothy Lynde Dix, known in her old age as Madam Dix, was "a typical example of the New England Puritan gentlewoman of the period,—dignified, precise, inflexibly conscientious, unimaginative, and without trace of emotional glow or charm."[3]

Elijah Dix moved his family to Boston in 1795 to Orange Court, a mansion in the heart of the city that Dr. Dix filled with beautiful French and English furniture, fine carpets, glass windows, silver candlesticks, and a library filled with books. He opened an apothecary shop—a drugstore—next to the city's famed Faneuil Hall. A shrewd businessman, Elijah Dix made many enemies. Eventually, his success in both medicine and real estate would prove to be not only Elijah Dix's undoing but his son's as well.

Joseph Dix and Mary Bigelow

One of eight children born to Elijah and Dorothy Dix, Joseph Dix was always considered delicate. By all accounts, his mother doted on him and his only sister, Mary. Most affluent families the time sent their sons to Harvard College. Joseph enrolled in the divinity school in 1794. He had difficulty adapting to college life and was dismissed in 1797 for receiving poor grades, leaving debts unpaid, and breaking college

Dorothea Dix's grandfather owned a pharmacy next door to Faneuil Hall (seen here), the famed building where patriots often held political meetings during the American Revolution.

rules. His father then sent him to Worcester, Massachusetts, where he was to receive training as a doctor. But Joseph failed at this, too. Then, in a moment of youthful rebellion, he married Mary Bigelow on January 28, 1801, causing his family—who had expected him to marry a wealthy, upper-class woman—great disappointment yet again.

Mary Bigelow had been born in Shrewsbury, Massachusetts, on July 15, 1779. She was the daughter of a sea captain. Her family's fortunes had risen and fallen by the time she met Joseph. For Mary, the marriage was an improvement in her social standing.

But the marriage only caused further tension between Joseph and his parents, who were growing tired of coming to his aid.

In order to avoid additional squabbles, Joseph and Mary Dix moved to Vermont to farm and manage a store. But Joseph was again unsuccessful, and the couple had to rely on Dr. Dix once more. This time, Joseph reluctantly signed on as the land manager of Dixmont Township, one of his father's two real estate ventures. In the early nineteenth century, New England was expanding rapidly. Dr. Dix had bought a large deal of land along the Penobscot River on the Massachusetts frontier—what is now Maine—and established two towns, Dixfield and Dixmont. His plan was to sell land to aspiring farmers, and he hoped that Joseph could manage that process.

Joseph, however, was unable to succeed at this enterprise—even in the face of a thriving real estate market. The final wedge between Joseph Dix and his parents came when he converted to Methodism and became a minister. A religion that believed life was a "savage struggle between the flesh and the spirit, between one's sinful nature and the redemptive, purifying power of God's grace," Methodism was "spreading like wildfire along the new nation's frontier."[4] While new ideas about culture and religion were prevalent in colonial America, Methodism was viewed with disdain by New England's prominent Congregationalists—such as the Dix family—who felt that Methodism was a crude, fire-and-brimstone religion.

The Minister's Daughter

As the daughter of a Methodist minister, Dorothea Dix felt the effects of her father's strict religion. She was encouraged to confess her faith and show repentance for her sins, and she was punished severely if she failed to do so. A strong-willed, independent child, a confession of faith ran against Dorothea's nature. The Methodist religion's "unbridled emotionalism," which included physically punishing disobedient children, and the fact that she was forced to spend hours sewing together religious pamphlets for her father, left Dorothea with a desire to escape her father's religion.

Joseph's dedication to his calling—and his wife's support of it—left Dorothea feeling neglected and unloved by her parents. By all accounts, her childhood was filled with hardship and unhappiness. "I never knew childhood!" she once wrote.[5] Her one source of happiness was the love she received from her grandfather Dix. Dorothea cherished the happy memories of the time she spent visiting her grandparents' home in Boston. Her grandfather took her with him in his carriage when he visited patients around Boston, and into his apothecary shop, teaching her about healing herbs and medicines.

However, Dorothea's happiness was cut short when Elijah Dix was murdered en route to Dixmont—some say by people who were unhappy about his land deals, others say by robbers—in 1809. His death left Madam Dix ashamed and aghast at the way her husband died,

Methodism

Methodism started in England in the 1700s. Led by John and Charles Wesley, both instructors at Oxford University, a group of men began meeting in 1729 to read and discuss the Bible. Their numbers grew, and they were soon called "Methodists."

Their literal interpretation of the Bible soon led to claims that they were too extreme. Because they defined their beliefs so narrowly, they thought few people were "good" enough to go to heaven. They believed human beings are sinful by nature, that people would be "saved" from going to hell by the strength of their faith, and that faith makes people holy. Their fiery sermons became quite popular and drew large crowds.

By 1735, John and Charles Wesley left England for Georgia, which was then under English rule. They intended to preach to and convert the American Indians. Through their efforts, Methodism began to take root in America.

One of the founders of Methodism, John Wesley moved to Georgia from England, then began to spread his teachings through America.

and the seven-year-old Dorothea lost the one person she felt loved her.

Putting further strain on the family, when Dorothea was ten, Mary Dix gave birth to a son, Charles Wesley, after the family had moved to Barnard, Vermont, to live near some of Mary Dix's relatives. To meet his growing family's needs, Joseph tried—and failed—to run a bookstore. The birth of Charles Wesley had put a strain on Mary Dix's health, and she became unable to care for the children. The responsibility now fell largely to Dorothea.

In 1815, Dorothea's brother Joseph was born, and the family moved to Worcester, where there were more business opportunities, as well as the aunts, uncles, and cousins of Madam Dix. However, Joseph Dix decided that he would continue his Methodist preaching in Worcester, in hopes of converting the townspeople.

Nearly thirteen years old, Dorothea had had enough. The pamphlet stitching, along with the responsibilities of caring for her brothers and running the household, had become overwhelming. Historians believe she ran away from home, taking a stagecoach from Worcester to Orange Court in Boston, where she pleaded with Grandmother Dix to let her stay. Even though Dorothea was her namesake, Grandmother Dix was nearly seventy. Caring for a teenager was likely a daunting task for the old woman. But Madam Dix had never approved of her son Joseph's Methodist religion or of Dorothea's mother, Mary Bigelow. She felt the child deserved a proper upbringing. Dorothea was allowed to stay.

3

LEARNING TO BE A LADY

If Dorothea Dix thought life at Orange Court would be easy, she quickly learned otherwise. The mansion held wonderful memories of her visits as a small child and of her grandfather's affection. It was filled with beautiful furniture and carpets, and it contained an entire library, which appealed to the bright young girl. But Madam Dix, who "placed duty above affection," took it upon herself to train Dorothea in the ways of society.[1] She would learn how to be a lady so that she could one day become a respectable and capable wife and mother. But Dorothea found the structure and discipline irritating, and Madam Dix felt that her granddaughter was stubborn and headstrong. The two soon began clashing regularly. As a result,

Dorothea felt she would never find the love she craved.[2]

Making the decision to leave her parents—especially for a young girl in 1815—was truly an act of bravery. It was highly unusual for a child to disobey her parents so forcefully. But Dorothea Dix was ready to detach herself permanently from Joseph and Mary Dix. She never saw them again. While she would spend the next several years moving between relatives in Boston and Worcester, she never lived with her parents. The break was not only physical but also psychological. In later years, she would even refer to herself as an orphan. There is some speculation that the hardships of her early childhood led to her deep compassion for the mentally ill.

Despite the quarrels with Madam Dix while at Orange Court, Dorothea Dix obtained an excellent education. Her aunt Mary's husband, Thaddeus Mason Harris, tutored her, along with lecturers from Harvard College. She also was allowed to use the Boston Public Library. She was an excellent student, and her academic accomplishments soon evolved into a desire to teach. Luckily, teaching was considered an appropriate occupation for a young lady of the time.

Madam Dix's health was beginning to fail, however. It was becoming too difficult for her to continue to oversee Dorothea's upbringing. After living at Orange Court for only two years, Dorothea was sent back to Worcester to live with her great aunt Sarah Lynde Duncan and Duncan's daughter, Sarah Fiske.

The city of Boston, as it looked during the years Dix lived there.

A New Home in Worcester

The two women were as warm and affectionate as Madam Dix was stern and proper. Under their care, Dix, who was now a young woman of fifteen, blossomed. She was described as "tall, erect, slight, good looking; neither very light nor very dark; with a round face and a very stern decided expression."[3]

By the time Dix moved in with her aunt, her parents had left Worcester for New Hampshire. For the first time, she was surrounded by cousins her own age. It was then that she began a close friendship with her cousin Edward Bangs. Some historians believe the two shared a romance. In Worcester, she was putting into practice the social graces Madam Dix had tried to force her to learn back at Orange Court.

The Dame School

Years of living in poverty and her Methodist upbringing made Dix feel she would never quite fit in. To compensate for her awkwardness, she convinced her aunt Sarah to allow her to open a school in Worcester in 1816. Called a dame school, it served as a source of primary instruction for little children. Still only a teenager, Dix attempted to make herself look older by wearing a long skirt and appearing very serious. Her students learned reading and writing, proper manners, and moral instruction—what is sometimes referred to today as character education, or ethics. The students also learned to sew.

Although Dix was a capable teacher, she tried to make up for her youth by being extremely strict with her students. Years later, one of her students recollected that she was a tough disciplinarian: "I don't know that she had any special grudge against me but it was her nature to use the whip and use it, she did."[4]

Dix embraced her role as a teacher and relished the authority associated with it. Two years after Dix began teaching, her parents sent her brother Charles Wesley to Worcester to live with the Duncans. He became one of Dix's pupils. Her brother Joseph soon followed. Dix once again took over parental responsibility for both of her brothers.

In spite of all their quarrels, Madam Dix missed her granddaughter. Around 1820, she requested that

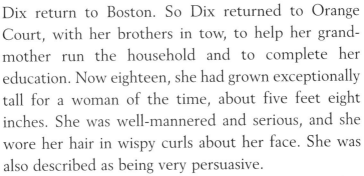

Dame Schools

A dame school was a small private school that taught working-class children before they were old enough to work. The students, mostly girls, were taught how to read and write. They also learned useful skills such as sewing. The students ranged in age from two to fifteen. Because they were not regulated by law, the schools' level of instruction varied widely. Some teachers were better than others. Sometimes students were expected to complete their lessons while the teacher did her housework. The schools were often run by elderly women who needed to supplement their family income.

Dix return to Boston. So Dix returned to Orange Court, with her brothers in tow, to help her grandmother run the household and to complete her education. Now eighteen, she had grown exceptionally tall for a woman of the time, about five feet eight inches. She was well-mannered and serious, and she wore her hair in wispy curls about her face. She was also described as being very persuasive.

Joseph Dix died in April 1821, bringing Dorothea a half-step closer to becoming the "orphan" she sometimes claimed to be. She had already written her parents out of her life, and she was apparently unmoved by the news of her father's death.

A Lifelong Friend

The most notable event in Dix's life around this time was her introduction to Anne Heath, who quickly became her closest friend, at the Hollis Street Church. Anne Heath was, in many ways, everything Dorothea Dix was not. Outgoing, Heath came from a large family that was warm and loving. At her home outside Boston in Brookline, Massachusetts, there was always a social event being talked about or planned. The two became fast friends. They became lifelong correspondents, and Heath's letters frequently cheered Dix and provided her with crucial support. Dix visited often, drawn to the happy family that she herself had always craved.

Back at Orange Court, Dix single-mindedly pursued her desire to run a school. Madam Dix finally permitted Dix to open a small day school for paying students within the mansion. Teaching was a source of great pride for Dix. "To me the avocation of a teacher has something elevating and exciting," she wrote to Anne Heath. Dix added, "What greater bliss than to look back on days spent in usefulness, in doing good to those around us, in fitting young spirits for their native skies."[5]

Dix soon decided that the most useful thing she could do would be to open a free school for poor children. During this time, New England was a place where ideas about education, religion, politics, and society were exchanged freely. It was not unusual for young, unmarried women like Dix to teach, especially since there were few other jobs open to them. It was also not unusual for a woman to be interested in philanthropy and social reform. Many wealthy and middle-class women used their free time to promote causes, such as temperance (opposition to alcoholic beverages) and abolition (the struggle against slavery).

Dix's next action was to persuade Madam Dix to allow her to open a charity school in the carriage house at Orange Court. In an attempt to convince her grandmother, Dix wrote:

> Had I the saint-like eloquence of our minister, I would employ it in explaining all the motives and dwelling on all the good, good to the poor, the miserable, the idle, and the ignorant, which would follow your giving me permission to use the barn chamber for a school-room for charitable and religious purposes. . . . [W]hy not, when it can be done without exposure or expense, let *me* rescue some of America's miserable children from vice and guilt? . . . Do, my dear grandmother, yield to my request, and witness next summer the reward of your benevolent and Christian compliance.[6]

In her letter, Dix appealed to her grandmother's sense of compassion. Madam Dix could not refuse such a heartfelt appeal. Dix was permitted to open her charity school. She named it the Hope School.

Becoming an Author

Striving to find her purpose in life, Dix continued her own education as well. She attended the many lectures and "conversations"—informal discussions on preassigned topics—that were the fashion at the time.

She even wrote her own "conversation," a manual for teachers to be used not only at the Hope School, but at private schools everywhere: *Conversations on Common Things; or, Guide to Knowledge: With Questions.* The book was published anonymously in 1824, when Dix was only twenty-two, a remarkable feat. Dix used a conversation between a mother and daughter as a basis for the book. *Conversations* became so popular that it remained in print until the early 1890s. One reviewer from the *United States Literary Gazette* wrote:

> We are gratified with finding an American writer who duly estimates the importance of giving to American children knowledge as will be actually useful to them, instead of filling their minds with vague . . . notions of subjects not accommodated to their age.[7]

Finding a New Religion

Dix was also becoming interested in Unitarianism, an emerging religion based on the belief that God exists within each individual person, and that a person lives in a world community where one takes social action. Dix began attending Dr. William Ellery Channing's sermons at his church on Federal Street. She wrote to Anne Heath that she was striving toward spiritual perfection so that she "might be a fit companion of the virtuous great . . . who 'tread the path of duty,' perfect in the way of righteousness."[8] A pious young woman, Dix took her quest for perfection very seriously. "Six faults must be abandoned by a man seeking prosperity," she wrote in her notebook, "sleep, drowsiness, fear, anger, laziness, loitering."[9]

Believing she was guilty of all six vices, Dix worked until she developed a chronic illness that was both mental and physical. She would work tremendously long hours, often teaching all day, attending a lecture in the evening, and then writing letters late into the night. As a result, she developed migraine headaches, lung infections, and a general weakness that, at times, left her partially paralyzed. Her illnesses often depressed her and, on recovery, she felt driven to work even harder. "I now think that you are sacrificing your life on what you conceive to be the altar of your duty," her friend Reverend John Pierpont once warned her.[10]

In 1825, Dix published a book of collected religious material, *Hymns for Children, Selected and Altered.* Meant to enrich the spiritual life of children, the book included bits of scripture, hymns, and moral tales from various religions—including Buddhism. This book, too, was well received. Dix began to believe that

Seen here as a young man, William Ellery Channing had a profound influence on Dorothea Dix and her life's work.

her purpose in life was to be a writer. That same year, she published another religious book. Called *Evening Hours*, it was a book of meditations for children.

Boston's religious community was taking notice of Dix's teaching and writing. Noting her work, Unitarian minister William Ellery Channing wrote to her, "I look forward to your future life not altogether without solicitude [protectiveness], but with a prevailing hope." Gently suggesting that she stop being so self-critical, he added: "You must learn to give up your plans of usefulness, as much as those of gratification, to the will of God."[11] Dix was flattered by his notice. Channing's friendship would have a lasting impact on her.

4

JOURNEYS OUTWARD

Philanthropy, or acts of charity for those in need, was increasingly becoming a focal point in Dix's life. She had not married by her late twenties, even though there were hints that she may have had a brief romance with her Worcester cousin Ed Bangs. Unlike other women of her time, her letters and notebooks indicate that she never seriously thought she would marry.

This was an unusual choice for a young woman in mid-nineteenth-century America. Women of the time were expected to marry and raise families. As a wife, Dix's life would have revolved around her private home—the domestic sphere. She would have been preoccupied with the concerns of running a household and raising a family. As a single woman, however, Dix would have more free time to do good works in the public eye.

Influences on Dix's Life

Dix's greatest influence was religion, specifically the Unitarian Church. It was common to take notes on the sermons given during church services, as Dix did, and to discuss their messages with other people. In the 1820s and 1830s, Unitarianism emphasized a person's spiritual oneness with God and the importance of performing good works. For Dix, Jesus Christ was a "man of action" who could heal the sick and feed the poor.[1] She would try to do the same.

Dix also had several personal sources of inspiration. William Ellery Channing, known as the father of Unitarianism, was widely regarded for his charismatic sermons. The sermons of Henry Ware, Jr., who spoke frequently on aiding the poor, were also a great inspiration. Especially influential was minister and activist Joseph Tuckerman, who took his ministry into the homes of the poor and downtrodden.

Joseph Tuckerman helped transform the American perception of poverty. His work with the poor began to dispel the myth that those who suffered hardships somehow deserved them. He preached that the poor were good people suffering from some misfortune—a woman whose husband had died, or a farmer whose crop had failed. In his view, such people deserved aid and compassion from those in a position to help.

Because Dix herself knew what poverty was like, Tuckerman's words struck a chord in her. She resolved to do her Christian duty by educating poor children. Observing Tuckerman's work in Boston, Dix saw first-hand how powerful the combination of human compassion and the resources of an established institution such as the church could be.

William Ellery Channing was so impressed by Dix that, in 1827, he invited her to accompany him and his family to their summer home, Oakland, in Newport, Rhode Island. Channing had a dedicated following of young people, and Dix considered him a mentor and father figure. She wrote of him to Anne Heath, "Near him you may suppose that anyone may, if they choose[,] be happy."[2] Dix served as a governess—a live-in tutor and caretaker—to the Channing children. She also organized a Sunday school on the estate

Boston's Reformers

There were many reform and social "movements" at the time that Dix could easily have joined. Just outside of Boston, in Cambridge, Massachusetts, Ralph Waldo Emerson, Henry David Thoreau, and Margaret Fuller were introducing Transcendentalism, which focused on intellectual and spiritual life. Bronson Alcott and Elizabeth Peabody were working to reform the state's education system. And the movement to end slavery, known as the abolition movement, led by William Lloyd Garrison, was beginning to take hold in New England. Dix, who had direct contact with Channing, Ware, and Tuckerman, began to follow their religious teachings.

Ralph Waldo Emerson was one of many prominent intellectuals living near Boston when Dix moved there.

grounds for local men and boys.

Dix had met another minister, named Ezra Stiles Gannett, in 1823. He was a recent graduate from Harvard Divinity School. He became a minister at William Ellery Channing's Federal Street Church, where Dix worshipped. Gannett and Dix began corresponding. When Dix decided to visit Philadelphia, Gannett provided her with letters of introduction to another Unitarian minister, William Henry Furness, the pastor of the First Congregational Unitarian Church of Philadelphia. Her visit there proved to be very important for Dix.

Furness also preached about the relationship between the church and an individual's social responsibility. His sermons caught her in the right frame of mind. Dix was more than ready to put the concept into practice.

In the spring of 1828, with Furness's blessing—he had just been selected to head the newly formed public school system—Dix began an inventory of dame schools throughout Philadelphia. Expanding her original plan, she also visited some of the schools run by

William Henry Furness, who headed the First Congregational Unitarian Church, influenced Dorothea Dix in the development of her theories about reform and society.

members of the Quaker religion, including one school for the deaf where she found children living in horrible conditions. They were dirty and wild. Dix was horrified, but after investigating further, she discovered that a reform movement was growing. Only one year earlier, the city had conducted its own investigation of the almshouses and work-houses, where poor people were put to work in exchange for food and housing. The study had assessed what kind of relief was available to the poor. The city's method of inspection—which included tours and interviews—would soon serve Dix well.

A Trip to the Virgin Islands

By 1830, Dix had become a part of the Channing household. She was still, however, helping Madam Dix run Orange Court and operating her own schools. All this activity was taking a toll on her health. She was suffering from exhaustion. When the Channings decided to travel to the Virgin Islands in the

Caribbean Sea in November 1830, Dix went with them in an attempt to restore her health.

Dix spent her time caring for the Channing children, walking along the beach, and exploring the island's unique plants and animals. She also saw slaves for the first time, working on the cotton and sugar plantations of the Virgin Islands. She spent some time strolling on the grounds of the plantation where she was staying with the Channing family, even stopping to ask the slaves questions.

When Dix returned to Boston in 1831, her health and vigor had returned. She decided to open another school. This time, her students came from elite families.

Ideas about school reform and the establishment of public schools for all children were becoming popular at the time. Dix, who was traveling more frequently in the reform-minded circles of the city's intellectuals, was right in the midst of the action.

Dix and Slavery

Surprisingly, Dix was unmoved by the plight of the slaves. Perhaps it was because Channing, whose family had owned slaves when he was a boy, was not active in the abolition movement. Or perhaps it was because Dix's passion lay elsewhere. She found the Virgin Islands romantic and believed that the slaves were well-cared-for heathens who should not be freed.[3]

As with her earlier school at Orange Court, Dix proved to be an exacting teacher, setting high standards for her students. She worked extremely hard and again exhausted her strength. This time, she was sure she was close to death.

By March 1836, she had sunk into a depression. Her friends, including Anne Heath and William Ellery Channing, as well as her doctor, encouraged her to travel to Europe as a way to improve her health. Dix decided to make the trip.

Recovery in Europe

Dix sailed for England in April 1836. She intended to travel on to France and Italy to soak up the sun and take in the sights. Instead, on her arrival in Liverpool, England, her health deteriorated to the point that she was coughing so much, she could not even sleep. Channing had given her a letter of introduction to his good friends, Elizabeth and William Rathbone III. Not knowing where else to turn, she wrote to them. They immediately came to her rescue. They brought her to their estate, Greenbank. There, she was able to rest and get better.

The Rathbones were wonderful to Dix. Social reformers themselves, their home was filled with progressive thinkers and artists. They were generous and compassionate. Dix spent months in bed fighting depression and pneumonia. She would appear in the evenings to discuss politics and social reform with William Rathbone.

As a man of stature in the community, Rathbone and his fellow reformers wanted to restructure existing English laws to establish a welfare system that would help those in need without creating a dependence on the government that would make them not want to work. The reformers' aim was to improve working conditions in the factories and living conditions in the prisons.

Dix was captivated by such talk. After she became strong enough, she began to research mental illness and discovered the role heredity might have played in her own bout of depression. She began to understand that some of her father's troubles may, in fact, have been caused by depression.

After her recovery, she visited what was considered England's most progressive insane asylum, the York Retreat. It was built in 1796 by William Tuke. The asylum looked like a private home. The patients there were treated very well, like guests. Doctors and scientists who were interested in the study of mental disorders and their treatment made a point of traveling to the asylum.[4] The asylum's philosophy was based on the principle that, if the mentally ill were treated with dignity and respect, and received compassionate care, they would recover fully. Physical restraints were seldom used, and isolation was viewed as unnecessary.

Dix's stay in England was a period of happiness that was marred only by the death of Madam Dix in the spring of 1837, followed by news of her mother's death. Dix did not return home in time to see her grandmother before her death, a decision for which her remaining family never completely forgave her.

She returned to Boston in the fall of 1837. By that winter, Madam Dix's estate had been settled. Dix's inheritance left her enough money—about $3,000 a year—to live comfortably for the rest of her life, with enough remaining for small charitable donations. The fact that she was a woman with money made her more powerful in the public sphere. As the years passed, she began using her wealth to open doors in the realm of politics, which was generally open only to men at the time.

After a few months in Boston, Dix grew restless. She was searching for something meaningful to do. By 1838, she felt stifled. Having lost Madam Dix, she felt she was truly without any family. She wrote in her diary: "I feel the event, as having divided the only link, save the yet closer one of fraternal bonds, which allies me to kindred."[5]

Embarking on Her Journey

Left with no real place to call home, Dix decided to travel. William Ellery Channing and Joseph Tuckerman had inspired her to engage in philanthropic work in Boston. But her trip to England had raised her interest not only in the humanitarian treatment of the mentally ill but also in the appropriate role government should play in this endeavor. Dix decided to move to Washington, D.C., to see what she could do. Rousing herself to action, she made a list: "The suffering—to be comforted;—the wandering led home . . . the indolent [lazy] roused; the over-excited restrained."[6]

Moving into a boardinghouse in Washington, D.C.'s Georgetown neighborhood, Dix began to visit the schools and orphanages of the city. She also began to visit the almshouses and jails, writing down all her observations as she went. These institutions were accessible to the public for a small fee, and Dix was allowed inside to observe as she pleased. At this point, however, she had no clear plan as to what she hoped to accomplish with all her careful note-taking.

Through her tours and research, Dix became keenly aware of the differences between asylums, prisons, and almshouses. This is the almshouse at Spruce Street in Philadelphia, Pennsylvania.

Unsure of her aims, she traveled from New York to Virginia to visit distant relatives. She felt physically renewed but found herself still searching for a purpose. Around this time, her brother Charles, who had become a sailor, was lost at sea and presumed dead. When news of her brother's loss reached her by the end of 1839, Dix felt ready to return to Boston once again.

5

STARTING HER LIFE'S WORK

At this point in her life, Dix was searching for a cause. Her social consciousness had been awakened during her trip to England. In some ways, she was ahead of her time. Boston's intellectuals were debating issues such as women's role in society, whether slavery should be abolished, and temperance. In Cambridge, Ralph Waldo Emerson, Henry David Thoreau, Margaret Fuller, and Bronson Alcott were developing Transcendentalist philosophy. But while their conversations and philosophical debates were important, Dix was looking for a way to take action.

When Harvard Divinity student John Nichols asked her if she knew of anyone who could take over his Sunday school class for the women inmates at the Middlesex County Jail in East Cambridge, Dix reportedly told him without hesitation, "I will take them [the women of the class] myself. . . . I shall be there next Sunday."[1]

The following Sunday, Dix taught an hour-long class to nearly twenty women. Afterward, she took a tour of the jail. She found nearly thirty mentally ill women, most of them dressed in rags and living in cells without heat.

There was something pitiful about these mentally ill prisoners that touched Dix. Seeing them alone and suffering, she found she could identify with them, after having suffered through and recovered from her own depression in England. She felt compelled to help. As she set out to inspect and inventory other jails, almshouses, and places where the insane were stashed away, she finally discovered what would become her life's work.

Dix Begins Her Inspection

Having the proper connections helped. Once again, Dix obtained letters of introduction, or credentials, from influential men—including her own doctor George Hayward, and Harvard Medical School's Walter Channing, a relative of the minister William Ellery Channing. These letters gained her admission to jails and asylums throughout the state.

Massachusetts had two asylums at the time: the Worcester State Lunatic Hospital, which opened in 1833, and the Boston Lunatic Hospital, which opened in 1839. Both were modeled after the York Retreat in England. They were based on the principles of moral

The Worcester State Lunatic Hospital in Massachusetts was one of the first places Dix visited in her crusade on behalf of the mentally ill.

treatment of the mentally ill. Dix had meetings with their administrators, interviewing them about treatment methods and recovery rates.

In the fall of 1841, she visited the Lowell Almshouse just outside Boston. She toured the building and grounds, asking questions about how the mentally ill were treated. She jotted her observations down in a notebook and began writing to other jail-keepers and almshouse operators throughout the state. As her journal of observations grew, so did her sense of purpose. The seeds of Dorothea Dix's memorial to the Massachusetts legislature had been planted. By the following year, her words would be read on the floor of the state legislature.

Dix had supporters in high places, men such as Horace Mann, a Massachusetts legislator who had helped found the Worcester Asylum, and the reformer and state legislator Samuel Gridley Howe. It was Howe who asked Dix to write her memorial, a petition to establish proper housing and care for the mentally ill. Howe's plan was to publish the address, distribute it throughout the state, and present it to the legislature when it met in January 1843. Dix, who was intelligent, authoritative, and certain that she was morally right in her cause, relished the challenge.

Memorial

By Christmas, 1842, Dix was nearly finished writing her memorial, which concluded with the request that the state build a new asylum for homeless people who were mentally ill. The memorial was sermon-like, and Dix drew on stark imagery that would win the compassion of those who heard it. Samuel Gridley Howe found it so stirring that he called for a special legislative session so it could be presented right away.

Horace Mann helped Dix in her efforts to get legislation through the Massachusetts state legislature.

Because women were not allowed to speak in the legislative chamber, Howe presented it for Dix. The legislators were so moved by her words that, in January 1843, a bill was introduced to expand the Worcester Asylum to make room for the poor insane.

Some people, however, were not impressed by Dix's crusade—especially the administrators of the hospitals she criticized. Many were outspoken in trying to refute Dix's claims. Initially, Dix would send harsh letters in response. But when her truthfulness was attacked by the newspapers, state Senator Charles Sumner rose to her defense. Sumner would later become a member of the United States Senate. He would champion the cause of the Union and abolition on the eve of the Civil War. Sumner asserted that he had seen the same conditions Dix described in the prisons. His testimony gave Dix credibility among the legislators and boosted her confidence and reputation.

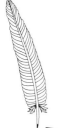

Criticism

While she may have won over the legislators whose votes she would need to achieve her goal, Dix's memorial alienated her from wardens and jailkeepers, many of whom had freely allowed her to enter their prisons. Some towns even published rebuttals, challenging the memorial's authenticity. A few town officials protested that Dix had spent only "five minutes" at their facilities and had taken no notes.[2]

Charles Sumner, a famous abolitionist and politician, would eventually become Dorothea Dix's champion in Congress.

Dix began to meet with individual legislators in an attempt to persuade them to support a bill. This practice, known as lobbying, would provide the Worcester Asylum with an additional $65,000—a huge sum of money at the time—for its construction.[3]

A New York Tour

Triumphant in her first success, Dix decided to broaden what was evolving into a crusade on behalf of the mentally ill. She traveled through New England and New York, visiting jails and almshouses, and chronicling her journeys in notebooks. Armed with her newfound reputation as a reformer, she could travel freely and no longer needed letters of introduction. By the fall of 1843, she was focusing exclusively on the state of New York. She published a memorial about conditions there in January 1844.[4]

An almshouse in Rome, New York, had several mentally ill women who had been sexually assaulted. In some instances, they had become pregnant as a result. This was all the evidence she needed to prove that it was not enough just to provide state funds to build asylums. A state-run system of care was necessary not only to cure these women but to protect them from harm. In her *Memorial to the Honorable the Legislature of the State of New York*, Dix began to develop the argument that the state itself should become the legal guardian of the mentally ill. Despite the fact that poor people who were mentally ill often wound up at almshouses because they had nowhere else to go, New York law did not actually permit this.

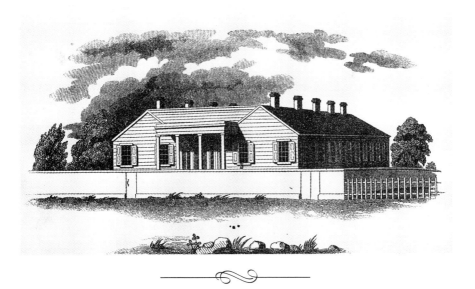

Dix did some of her earliest work trying to improve conditions in women's asylums in New York, like the Magdalen Female Benevolent Asylum, seen here.

With the support of New York Governor William Seward, Dix proposed that the asylum being built on a 130-acre plot of land in Utica, New York, be expanded for the poor.[5] Lawmakers had already discussed the topic at great length during the late 1830s. Dix ultimately had little direct impact there, but her presence helped keep the process moving.

Further Travels

While the New York legislature debated whether to expand the Utica asylum, as eventually was done, Dix was off to inspect facilities in Rhode Island, New Jersey, and Pennsylvania. She traveled the country at a time when it was unusual for a woman to travel alone and when few major roadways existed. The most popular method of travel was by train. But since she made it a habit of traveling throughout the most remote parts of each state, she often ended up traveling by wagon or boat. When asked years later if she was ever afraid while traveling alone, Dix said, "I am naturally timid and diffident, like all my sex; but in order to carry out my purposes, I know that it is necessary to make sacrifices and encounter dangers." She went on to describe one incident that occurred while she was in the state of Michigan. Realizing that her wagon driver was carrying a set of pistols out of fear of being robbed, she told him, "Give me the pistols,—I will take care of them." Soon after, a man came rushing out of the woods, intending to steal Dix's purse. Dix recalled, "I said to him, with as much self-possession as I could command, 'Are you not ashamed to rob a woman?'" The man grew pale, saying, "My God, that voice!" He proceeded to tell Dix that, while she was touring the Philadelphia penitentiary, he had heard her speak. She gave the man some money and sent him on his way.[6]

Moving on to Rhode Island

In Rhode Island, Dix became more fully engaged in the legislative process. The state was not yet officially involved in caring for the mentally ill. Current law provided that "furiously mad persons dangerous to the peace and safety of the good people" could be imprisoned in the county jails, while those less dangerous were confined to their homes to be cared for by family members or sent to the almshouse.[7]

Nicholas Brown, founder of the prestigious Brown University, had left the state $30,000 at the time of his death to establish an asylum for the mentally ill. However, the state did not establish the Rhode Island Asylum for the Insane until January 1844.[8]

By the time Dix traveled to Rhode Island, she had made it her mission not only to chronicle what she saw in the almshouses, but to lobby the state legislature to establish a "lunacy commission" to review formally the plight of the mentally ill. After Dix highlighted one particular case, that is exactly what the legislators did.

Dix wrote publicly about her visit to Abraham Simmons, a man who was kept chained to the floor in a stone-cold cell. Dix visited him in the town of Little Compton, Rhode Island, on a wintry day. After asking why Simmons was kept in such a cold place—and chained—the woman caretaker said, "Sometimes he screams dreadfully and that is the reason we had the double walls and the two doors. His cries disturb us in the house."

After Dix asked how long the man had been imprisoned in such a way, the woman replied, "Oh, above three years."

When Dix commented on the icy temperature in the cell, the woman spoke of the man as if Simmons were an animal, saying that her husband frequently "rakes out half a bushel of frost, and yet he [Simmons] never freezes."[9]

Believing strongly that mentally ill people deserved compassionate treatment, Dix entered Simmons's cell and began talking to him softly and kindly. She turned her anger into action by writing of his plight in the *Providence Journal*. She embarrassed his caretakers by making it known that he was kept a virtual prisoner:

> Should any persons in this philanthropic age be disposed from motives of curiosity to visit the place they may rest assured that traveling is considered quite safe in that part of the country, however improbable it may seem. The people of the region profess the Christian religion, and it is said that they have adopted those forms and ceremonies which they call worship. It is not probable, however, that they address themselves to poor Simmons' God. Their worship mingling with the prayers of agony which he shrieks from his dreary abode, would make a strange discord in the ear of the Almighty Being in whose keeping sleeps the vengeance due to all his wrongs.[10]

Relating the story of Abraham Simmons, Dix aggressively approached other wealthy Rhode Island merchants, hoping to get enough funding to complete and operate a mental hospital. She met first with Cyrus Butler, a seventy-eight-year-old bachelor who was reported to have millions of dollars. He already knew of Dix, and when she came to his office, said, "Are you Miss Dix? If so, sit down." Dix sat and told him the story of how she had found Abraham Simmons chained in a freezing shed. Butler said, "What do you wish me to do?"

Dix replied, "To subscribe $50,000 for the enlargement of your asylum and let it be called henceforth the 'Butler Hospital.'"[11]

"I will give $40,000 provided $40,000 more shall be obtained from other sources or shall be subscribed by responsible persons within six months from April first," Butler said. He added, "Furthermore, there should remain a sum not less than $50,000 as a permanent fund whose income should be applied solely on the support of the institution."[12]

For one person to donate forty thousand dollars in 1840 was extraordinary generosity. Some state legislatures did not even provide so much money for Dix's cause. For Dix even to ask for $50,000 from one person, and actually to get close to that amount, took a great deal of courage—courage she found she could easily muster. She had accomplished single-handedly in one meeting what the state legislators had been avoiding for the last few years—finding an appropriate funding source for the asylum.

Spurred on by her success with Cyrus Butler, Dix took her case to the Rhode Island legislature once more to ask for the other $40,000. Because, as a woman, she was not allowed to speak for herself in the legislature, she provided the members with the report she had written for the *Providence Journal* on Abraham Simmons. Members of the legislature were so moved that they agreed to provide the additional money.

A Warm Welcome in New Jersey

After accomplishing her aim in Rhode Island, Dix planned to focus next on New Jersey and Pennsylvania. New Jersey lawmakers were eager to meet her. Her reputation as a dedicated and thorough reformer preceded her.

As she traveled throughout New Jersey and Pennsylvania, Dix made the transition from social reformer and crusader to lobbyist. She began drafting legislation herself, based on her investigations. At a time when women could not own property or vote, she was recognized as a one-woman political force. Her intelligence and persistence on the issue of the mentally ill were widely respected.

New Jersey did not have any system in place for treating the mentally ill, and Dix was heartily welcomed as an expert who could lead the way. By now, she knew how to work within the system. She met with the governor right away and enlisted his support. In her statewide survey, she explained that the number of uncared-for mentally ill people outnumbered the entire prison population.

Dix's memorial to the New Jersey legislature showed her growing sophistication as an activist. Instead of conveying only her impressions of what she saw, she also incorporated aspects of official reports and inventories made by state commissioners in 1839. She wrote,

> I do not come here to quicken your generous impulses, and move you to emotion, by showing the existence of terrible abuses, revealing scenes of almost incredible sufferings. I come to ask justice of the Legislature of New Jersey, for those who, in the providence of God, are incapable of pleading their own cause, and of claiming redress for their own grievances.[13]

Dix included descriptions of humane treatments for the mentally ill, discussed their various success rates, and described what a hospital built for the sole purpose of caring for the insane could do. She also appealed to the legislators' compassion:

> Have you human feelings, can you delay this work which is solicited for the benefit of those who are . . . emphatically your wards, the wards of the state; for whose condition hereafter you are certainly accountable—inasmuch as you are largely able to provide a refuge . . . for the diseased, as their forlorn condition requires?[14]

Her experience in New Jersey marked her evolution from someone who was simply reporting what she had seen, to one who took action in support of her cause. She wrote to her friend Harriet Hare: "I am so tired I can hardly hold my pen. . . . Some evenings I have at once twenty gentlemen for three hours, steady conversation."[15] After one state representative claimed that the "wants of the insane in New Jersey were all humbug," Dix spoke for nearly an hour on the atrocities she had seen in his own district. The daring move won his support. He told her:

> I do'nt for my part want to hear anything more; the others can stay here if they want to; I am convinced, and you've conquered me out and out; I shall vote for the Hospital; if you'll come to the House and talk there as you've done here, no man that is'nt a brute can withstand you; and so when a man's convinced that's enough.[16]

Dix's memorial requested that the state erect a hospital for the insane. After only three weeks of debate, her proposal was adopted by the state legislature and signed by the governor on March 25, 1845.[17] Although it took the state three years to build and open the hospital near Trenton, Dix would refer to it as her "first-born child," since it was the first hospital founded as a result of her efforts.[18]

Success in Pennsylvania

While she remained active in establishing the New Jersey asylum, Dix moved into Pennsylvania. Dix once again lobbied for a state hospital, touring the jails and almshouses in an effort to complete her Pennsylvania *Memorial Soliciting a State Hospital for the Insane*

The hospital for the mentally ill at Trenton, New Jersey, was the one Dix considered her "first born."

quickly. After touring so many prisons and poor houses, Dix was becoming an expert on the nature of the institutions themselves—how they should be organized and operated and what was considered a prison, almshouse, or asylum. She noted that Pennsylvania, the state with the most organized prison system in the country, had a terrible method of treating the insane. They were either sent to almshouses or auctioned off to someone who would provide minimum care for them at the lowest cost and be reimbursed by the state—a sort of foster care system with no real oversight.

As she had done in Rhode Island, Dix lobbied the state legislature for a minimal amount of money to get work started on a public hospital for the insane. She settled for a mere $15,000 from the legislature, which Governor Francis Shunk signed into law on April 14, 1845.[19] She set out to raise another $15,000, which would be enough to construct a simple hospital. She considered this a small triumph. Philanthropist James Lesley told her that "no man nor woman, other than yourself, from Maine to Louisiana could have passed the bill under the discouraging circumstances with which you had to contend."[20]

At this point, she also became involved in choosing hospital sites in both New Jersey and Pennsylvania, and she worked with the architects to design a hospital that would provide a nurturing—some said opulent—atmosphere for the mentally ill. She worked with a group of prominent philanthropists she had brought together to select the land and oversee construction on the hospital, which began in 1849.

Continuing Her Work

Remarkably, while she lobbied the state legislatures in New York, Rhode Island, New Jersey, and Pennsylvania, Dix also found the time to travel to Ohio, Indiana, and Illinois. During the summer of 1844, she traveled throughout the Midwest, making her rounds among the prisons and almshouses and taking her inventories. She also went south, to Baltimore, Maryland, and Richmond, Virginia. By late 1845, Dix had traveled more than ten thousand miles and had visited eighteen state prisons, three hundred county jails, and more than five hundred almshouses and other institutions.[21]

Dorothea Dix spent the next five years traveling alone throughout the southern United States, achieving major victories on behalf of the mentally ill in Alabama, Kentucky, Tennessee, North Carolina, South Carolina, and Georgia. "I have been so happy as to promote and secure the establishment of six hospitals for the insane, several county poorhouses, and several jails on a reformed plan," she wrote to her friend Elizabeth Rathbone in England.[22] She wrote Mrs. Rathbone again a few years later, saying of her successes: "Shall I not say to you, dear friend, that my uniform success and influence are evidence to my mind that I am called by Providence to the vocation to which life, talents, and fortune have been surrendered these many years?"[23]

Surprisingly, Dix's health did not fail her through her long, hard hours of work, as it had so often while she was still a young school teacher and aspiring reformer back in Boston. Perhaps Dix was simply too busy to allow herself to become ill.

After her victories, large and small, she decided that the United States needed more than the state hospitals she had helped establish in her crusade. The time had come to make a plea for a federal system of hospitals for the mentally ill. Dix would be the one to take that message to Congress and to the president himself.

6

TO THE CAPITOL!

By 1847, Dix was probably one of the country's most effective lobbyists and reformers. While Northern abolitionists and Southern slaveholders were clashing over the issues of slavery and secession—whether the Southern states would band together and form their own country, denying their ties to the United States—Dix avoided the debate. She had never been particularly moved by the abolition movement. Her feelings on the issue are somewhat unclear. She did make extensive contacts with prominent people in the South, many of them wealthy plantation—and slave—owners, who would donate to her cause. She remained focused on providing care and treatment for the mentally ill.

At a time when lawmakers in Washington, D.C., were preoccupied with the issue of slavery, Dix took her cause to the nation's capital. After traveling widely observing—and creating—many different state policies on "lunacy reform," as her cause was then called, Dix began to believe that a standard policy at the national level made the most sense. Her goal was to establish a national asylum for the mentally ill.

In 1847, she decided to lobby members of Congress for a land grant—acres of land on which an asylum could be built. "They say, 'Nothing can be done here!'" Dix wrote to Harriet Hare. "I reply, 'I know no such word in the vocabulary I adopt!'"[1]

An Uphill Battle

Dix embarked on her most difficult task yet. Her experience so far had been very positive. She had met with success at every turn, and quickly—sometimes in just a matter of weeks. But working with Congress and the president would be her biggest challenge. Not only would she have to contend with many competing interests, but she would have to become familiar with the process of national politics.

Dix would face many obstacles. For example, a bill might be introduced and passed in the House of Representatives. The Senate could then expand on the legislation passed by the House, requiring the two chambers to agree on the new version before sending it to the president. In Congress there were more people with whom she would have to negotiate. Senators represented the interests of a state, whereas members

A view of the United States Senate chamber as it looked during Dix's time. As a lobbyist, Dorothea Dix became well aware of the Senate's inner workings.

of the House of Representatives came from a portion of a state. Dix would have to deal with people representing many different interests. Then, after carefully negotiating with both chambers of Congress, Dix's bill might still face a presidential veto. Legislation could be rejected by the president and returned to the House of Representatives, where the entire process would begin all over again. To win her case, she knew she would have to garner support at every turn.

Undaunted, Dix presented her memorial to Congress in June 1848. It requested that 5 million acres of federal land be set aside for asylums for the mentally ill. Her plan was to allocate a parcel of land to each state. The state would then be responsible for building and operating its own hospital.

Although 5 million acres was a huge amount of land, Dix felt justified in her request. At the time, railroads and universities were receiving many land grants from the government. By 1845, 5 million acres of federal land had already been granted to the states, and there was plenty more available. Dix felt that her 5 million was just a drop in the bucket.[2]

For the next six years, Dix walked back and forth between the two chambers of Congress, lobbying the members for support. Initially, she received little attention. Members of Congress were mainly focused on the "intensifying sectional conflict that had become more bitter with the close of the Mexican War."[3] That conflict between the United States and Mexico occurred from 1846 to 1848. It was driven by a desire to expand American borders. When the United States won, it took vast amounts of western land from Mexico. By the end of the war, tensions in Congress had begun to rise over whether slavery would be permitted in these new territories.

Day after day, Dix sat in the Senate gallery, as women were allowed to do. She listened as lawmakers gave speech after speech about slavery but agreed on nothing. She began to develop a low opinion of these lawmakers. She wrote to a friend that they possessed "so much apathy and so strange want [lack] of a consistent and wise policy," that she wondered how could they possibly get anything accomplished or solve any problems.[4]

A Point of Agreement

In Dix's view, the issue of caring for the mentally ill should be something on which the lawmakers *could* agree. Who could say that mentally ill individuals did not deserve to be fed, clothed, and provided with proper shelter at the very least? Up to this time, each state government had been primarily responsible for caring for its own citizens. Dix argued that a new system should be started on the national level, and the federal government was in the best position to accomplish that goal.

She believed the issue would allow lawmakers to feel as if they were accomplishing something worthwhile, even as they struggled in vain over the slavery issue. They could put aside any differences they may have had on the slavery issue and forge a consensus on caring for the mentally ill.

Dix was unyielding in her aim. She forced the members of Congress to pay attention to the issue of the insane.

Dix's federal memorial, *Memorial of D. L. Dix Praying a grant of land for the relief and support of the indigent curable and incurable insane in the United States*, included a nationwide inventory of the mentally ill. She argued that caring for the mentally ill made moral and economic sense. *"About eleven twelfths of all the insane who absolutely require fostering and remedial care are wholly unprovided for in this country,"* she wrote.[5] Using figures from the 1840 census, Dix launched into descriptions of particularly troubling cases she had encountered in nearly every state, including a mentally ill man in Maine who "had torn out his eyes" and a New Hampshire woman who was kept in a cage so small that "she grew double" and was reduced to walking on all fours.[6] Dix even mentioned the Simmons case from Rhode Island to bolster her point that federal intervention was necessary.

While Dix had decided during the time she spent working with the Pennsylvania legislature that the mentally ill should be made legal wards of their state—meaning that the state government would be responsible for their care and safekeeping—she now argued that they should be made "wards of the nation."[7] Calling upon all the moral authority she could muster, Dix rallied the members of Congress to put aside their divisive arguments about slavery and see themselves as part of one nation.

Her allies were those senators from states in which she had already been successful, such as Rhode Island, Massachusetts, Tennessee, Kentucky, and Pennsylvania. Tennessee Senator John Bell and Kentucky Senator Gerrit Davis welcomed Dix's presence in Washington. Largely due to her reputation as a reformer, when Dix presented her petition to the Senate, it was not simply assigned to an existing committee, where it might have been lost in the shuffle of competing issues. Instead, a special committee was formed to study it and decide whether legislation should be drafted. At

Dix's request, Missouri Senator Thomas Hart Benton served as chairman of the special committee. He agreed to introduce her memorial formally as a bill. However, Benton soon had second thoughts about such a grand proposal. The bill was introduced instead by New York Senator John Adams Dix, who was no relation to the social reformer.

Dorothea Dix worked closely with the senators to pass the bill, known as S. 328. She was granted special privileges in the Senate. She had a special desk reserved for her in the Senate library where she could work and write. No woman before had ever been granted such a great privilege, nor had a woman been treated as an equal by these powerful statesmen.

By the summer of 1848, the bill Dix was urging had been modified to include an allocation of "first five and then ten million acres of the public domain as

a special reserve that could be gradually sold off to finance 'a perpetual fund for the care of the indigent insane.'"[8] The objective was simply to allocate the land and not request any federal money. The special

Senator John Adams Dix was one of Dix's strongest supporters in Congress.

Senate committee unanimously passed the bill on July 21, 1848.

Dix's quest now was to get the bill passed by the full Senate, and then to move to the House of Representatives in the hope that it would be quickly approved there. But once again, slavery and the issue of states' rights overshadowed Dix's efforts.

How a Bill Becomes a Law

Legislation, also referred to as a bill, is introduced and read on the floor of either the House of Representatives or the Senate by a sponsor. Bills are usually introduced first in the House, but this is not necessary for all bills. The bill is then assigned to a committee. The Labor and Education Committee, for example, would consider bills that have to do with school and employment issues.

The committee may hold public hearings, where committee members hear statements for and against a bill. After this, they may make changes to it and then vote to send it to the chamber floor, where it is debated and possibly passed. If one house of Congress passes the bill, it is sent to the other chamber, where it goes through the same process.

Once the bill has been passed by both the House of Representatives and the Senate, members from both chambers meet in a conference to agree to changes to the bill. After both the House and Senate agree to the final bill, it is sent to the president to sign. Once the president signs it, the bill becomes a law.

Having been eclipsed by the slavery issue, as well as the Mexican War, Dix's bill had gone nowhere by the end of the congressional session in 1849. She would have to start the entire process again the following year.

Persuasion

Dix continued to view her plan as both practical and necessary. However, her single-mindedness would ultimately be her undoing in Washington. Horace Mann—her former champion in the Massachusetts legislature, and now a member of the House of Representatives—wrote to his wife in the winter of 1849: "Miss Dix is here laboring with all her might, but it is a matter of doubt where she will accomplish any thing during this session."[9]

Mann was right. She would not accomplish anything. But she did sow the seeds of reform among the senators, cultivating relationships wherever she could, calling on the men to listen to her arguments of moral persuasion. As a woman, she was excluded from the inner workings of Washington deal making. She could not sit up late at night with the men, talking over a bottle of wine. Instead, she attempted to persuade the men that, by supporting her proposal, they would be doing something good for humankind. She found an ally in the idealistic Massachusetts Senator Charles Sumner, who was primarily interested in ending slavery but supported her bill on its own merits of philanthropy. New York Senator John Adams Dix and Vice President Millard Fillmore—with whom she would strike up a lengthy correspondence—also supported her efforts, as did Massachusetts Senator Daniel Webster.

When Congress convened in January 1850, Horace Mann recommended that Dix revise her memorial, making the request for land slightly smaller. She would need to reintroduce the bill, at the very least, since legislation was not permitted to carry over from one session of Congress to the next. Mann became Dix's ally in the House of Representatives. When her new petition was ready in August 1850, he officially introduced it for her as bill H.R. 383.

Only a month earlier, President Zachary Taylor had died while in office. Her good friend Vice President Millard Fillmore had replaced him. At first, Dix was disappointed that she would have to start all over, lobbying the new president. However, she soon realized that, because of their friendship, Fillmore would be more likely to sign the legislation when Congress sent it to him.

The Argument for a National Hospital

In this new congressional session, Dix found that she ran the risk of falling "victim to her own success"— several Southern senators argued that, since the states were doing such a fine job with their own hospitals, no federal help was necessary.[10] And when it came time for real debate on the issue, many senators were wary of how such a large land grant would work. New England contained very little federal land and was reluctant to give up any of it to the mentally ill. States

President Millard Fillmore, a close friend of Dix's, showed great support for her efforts to establish government-run hospitals for the mentally ill.

with large parcels of federal land felt sure that they would be required to allocate it for Dix's purposes.

By 1851, the bill had passed in the Senate but failed in the House. At the same time, her political clout could not have been any greater. President Fillmore liked Dix, and she, in turn, provided him with insight into which senators were likely to support his proposals. It was Fillmore who encouraged her to persevere. "Hope on—Hope ever! My philosophy is, that all things are for the best," he declared. He added, "rest assured, that where we have done our duty, God will eventually bless our work."[11] As she told the president, she was "Defeated but not conquered."[12]

Dix decided to do what she did best: travel around checking on the progress of her hospitals and lobbying the states to build new ones. For the next three years, she traveled north to Canada, establishing hospitals and advocating for reform from Nova Scotia and Prince Edward Island to Montreal, and back south again. Her efforts were marked by one particular instance of goodwill in Nova Scotia.

Canadian Travels

After going to Sable Island, Dix heard the story of how, the day after her visit, a ship called *The Guide* had sunk in a thick fog. Although no one had died, Dix had noted that the island had no lifeboats or emergency fogbells. There was not even a lighthouse to help steer a ship to safety.

Acting quickly, Dix established a Sable Island lifeboat fund among her philanthropist friends. Six new lifeboats were soon placed on the island for use in emergencies. Touched by her action, the Nova Scotia Parliament (legislature) decided to take a second look at Dix's asylum bill, which called for an appropriation of over $60,000. The bill passed easily.[13]

A Small Success but a Larger Failure

Back in Washington, D.C., and frustrated by Congress's lack of action, in 1852, Dix persuaded President Fillmore to establish the Army and Navy Hospital for the Insane—known today as St. Elizabeth's—via executive order. This meant that the president could simply issue the order, effectively bypassing the congressional process that had frustrated Dix for so long.

Through her skillful political maneuverings, Dix was able to get Dr. Charles Nichols, a doctor she had handpicked, to run the facility. She also convinced President Fillmore that the hospital should be regulated by the Department of Interior—because that department monitored the use of federal land—as opposed to the Department of the Army.

Dix continued to lobby Congress on behalf of her land grant bill. In March 1854, it passed the Senate once again. Dix wrote to Heath, "My bill has passed the Senate by more than two-thirds majority. . . . It is now before the House and Congratulations flow in. . . . And as I rejoice quietly and silently, I feel it is *The Lord who has made my mountain to stand strong.*"[14]

But as the news reached her that the bill passed the House, the new president, Franklin Pierce, who had by this time succeeded Millard Fillmore, was rumored to be contemplating a veto. A veto would make all of Dix's efforts moot. Once a bill is vetoed, it returns to the House and Senate. If the legislature wishes to override the veto, the bill must be passed a second time—by a two-thirds majority. While Dix's bill passed in the Senate with such a large cushion, it did not in the House.

President Franklin Pierce was not an ally. He vetoed Dix's bill on the very day it passed the House. He stated that Congress did not have the authority to establish hospitals outside the District of Columbia—the nation's capital—and that the bill would wrongly impose the power of the federal government over the states. As Pierce explained, "If Congress have power to make provision for indigent insane *without the limits of this district*, it has the same power to provide for the indigent who are not insane and thus to transfer to the

After Fillmore left office, Dorothea Dix faced the task of getting her plans past the new president, Franklin Pierce (seen here). Unlike Fillmore, Pierce was not a Dix supporter. He vetoed her land grant bill.

federal government the charge of *all the poor in all the States.*"[15] If Congress could impose its will on the states with regard to the care of the poor insane, then the federal government would be responsible for all the poor people in the country. President Pierce did not see this possibility as a good idea.

The veto override attempt occurred in July. It failed. No longer a stranger to politics, Dix was outraged. She claimed President Pierce "was undoubtedly drunk" when he vetoed the bill.[16] She would later allege that it was Secretary of War Jefferson Davis, a Southerner who sympathized with states' rights issues and would later become president of the Confederacy, who objected to the bill for his own selfish purposes. Completely disheartened and physically exhausted, Dix decided to take a break from political wrangling. She left for Europe to visit her good friends the Rathbones.

Home to Greenbank

In need of rest after years of speaking, persuading, lobbying, and having no real place to call home, Dix left for England in the fall of 1854. The Rathbones welcomed her back to Greenbank as if she were a family member.[17] She found the estate almost unchanged.

Never one to be still for long, however, Dix soon found herself drawn into the prevailing issue of the day: England's poor. She began inspecting English workhouses, much as she had spent the last fifteen years inspecting jails and almshouses in America. Before long, she was once again politically engaged in the issue of caring for the mentally ill, this time in England, Scotland, and Ireland.

For a woman of fifty-two, Dix set a remarkable pace, scouring the countryside for indigent insane and charming her way into existing hospitals and asylums. Although the British Parliament had established a "lunacy reform commission," there remained much to be done. Dix intended to help the commissioner, Anthony Ashley Cooper, the seventh Earl of Shaftesbury, do it.[18]

After spending a few months in Switzerland with the Rathbones, Dix went next to France, visiting

This map shows some of the places Dix visited on her tour of Europe.

hospitals in Paris, Quilly, Rouen, St. Yan, Orleans, Nantes, and Tours. Then she made her way to Italy.[19]

Dix spent approximately two weeks in Naples, Italy. She was quite pleased by the care the hospitals there offered to the mentally ill. This was not the case in Rome, however. Dix was so mortified by what she found in the hospitals there that she demanded—and got—a meeting with Pope Pius IX, to tell him exactly what she had seen. Using the same vivid descriptions that had moved so many American legislators, Dix described the conditions of the hospitals and pleaded for improvements. The pope was so moved by her stories of the suffering patients that he called her a saint.[20] According to legend, the pope himself visited the same hospital wards the next day and vowed to make improvements.

Dix swept through Europe, a one-woman crusade for the mentally ill. She moved north through Italy, then traveled to Greece, and even went as far east as Turkey—an astonishing feat for one woman to do alone at the time. Instead of spending her time leisurely strolling through these countries' beautiful tourist attractions, Dix wandered through hospital wards, visiting the sick and trying to ensure that they were being well provided for. It was almost as if her failure in Washington, D.C., had made her more determined to see that the mentally ill were being properly cared for, not only in America but throughout the world.

7

BACK HOME, BACK TO WAR

Dix returned home to the United States in March 1857. James Buchanan had become president, and sectional tensions were simmering to a boil. The country was on the brink of war after years of divisive debate over slavery and states' rights. Dix hoped to regroup, pay visits to her friends, and check on the progress of her hospitals.

Doctors at the time were developing new theories regarding the treatment of the mentally ill. There was a move away from the presumption that mental illness could be cured with the proper treatment, a theory in which Dix herself believed, and a move toward the theory that it was a chronic, or lifelong, illness. The new theory reopened the question of whether hospitals should establish separate wards for long-term-care patients.

When Dix tried to pass a measure through the New York legislature in 1857 that would set up a separate hospital for chronically ill patients, it failed miserably. The public had turned its attention to other issues—most of them economic—and had lost interest in the care of the ill. Dix's one triumph during these years came in 1859, when the hospital Dix had fought to establish in Pennsylvania was named Dixmont Hospital in her honor.

Continuing Her Work

Without a permanent home to call her own, Dix once again took up traveling. In 1859 alone, she traveled through at least a dozen states. During her trips, she inspected facilities, made appropriations requests to state legislatures, and generally made sure that her plan was progressing. She traveled tirelessly, spending January in Pennsylvania, Maryland, North Carolina, and South Carolina. By February, she had moved into Georgia. She spent time in Louisiana and Texas in March and April. In May, she was in Tennessee and Missouri. By June, she was back north, in Illinois, Ohio, Pennsylvania, and New Jersey. In July, she spent time in Baltimore, Maryland, then went to Boston and farther north to Canada. By the winter of 1860, she was back in the Deep South.[1]

Dix seemed to refuse to stay in one place. She was driven by her cause, and she may have been afraid to slow down. By now, she had grown frail, and although she continued to have lung trouble, she seemed to have no desire to stop traveling and working.

The Road to War

Dix was in Mississippi in October 1859 when militant abolitionist John Brown stormed the arsenal at Harpers Ferry, Virginia (now part of West Virginia), and tried to begin a mass slave rebellion. Although the uprising was put down, tensions between the North and South had reached a breaking point. In November 1860, when Northerner Abraham Lincoln was elected president, the South prepared to leave the Union.

No longer could Dix ignore the issue of slavery or the role it had played in the debate over her land grant bill. Despite her passionate—and compassionate— attitude toward the issue of the mentally ill poor, there was a part of her that could not understand why slavery and states' rights were tearing the country apart. When South Carolina declared that it was seceding from the Union in December 1860, Dix wrote to Anne Heath from Washington, "I have never read anything in the history of any people more extra-ordinary than that which is characterizing the people of the gulf states" of Louisiana, Alabama, Mississippi, and Texas.[2]

To Dix, it seemed the South was "*determined* on a *Revolution*," but she would do her best to keep focused on her work for as long as she could.[3] She spent the winter of 1860 in Kentucky, working to provide funds to rebuild the Ward Hospital she had founded, which had recently burned down. War might be coming, but she had work to do.

By February 1861, Dix was asked to return to Springfield, Illinois, the state's capital, to lobby for additional funds for the state's Hospital for the Insane, which she had helped found back in 1847. She achieved a surprisingly easy victory: The state legislature agreed to provide the additional money. It also passed a bill drafted by Dix, which included additional money she felt was necessary. She wrote to Anne Heath, "I thank God, dear Annie, I have such full uses for time now, for the state of our beloved country, otherwise, would crush my heart and life."[4]

The Civil War

Despite her lack of interest in the issues that led to the fighting, Dix would play a pivotal role in the American Civil War. She organized a female nursing brigade and even—legend has it—waylaid an attempt to cut off Washington, D.C., from the rest of the North by burning the railroad bridges and assassinating the newly elected President Lincoln on his way to Washington. Samuel Felton, the president of the Philadelphia and Baltimore Railroad, told the story: In early 1861, Dix paid a visit to him at his office and "put in a tangible and reliable shape by the facts she related what before I had heard in numerous and detached parcels."[5] Felton went on to say that, while traveling in the South, Dix had overheard a plot to "seize upon Washington, with its archives and records, and then declare the Southern Confederacy . . . the

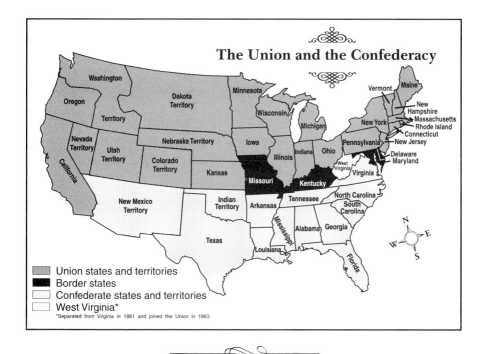

The United States were divided in loyalty between the Northern Union and the Southern Confederacy during the Civil War.

Government of the United States." The plot entailed cutting the railroad lines between Washington and the north, west, and east. Lincoln's inauguration was to be prevented and an attempt on his life would be made.[6] Felton believed Dix, and immediately hired detectives to act as spies in the South. The story turned out to be true. As a result, Felton smuggled President Lincoln through to Washington, evading the assassins and allowing Lincoln to be inaugurated safely and on schedule.

Heeding the Call

War broke out in April 1861 when Confederate soldiers fired on Fort Sumter in Charleston, South Carolina. At the time, Dix was staying with Horace Buttolph and his wife at the New Jersey State Lunatic Hospital. All around her, men were heeding President Abraham Lincoln's call to enlist as Union soldiers. Although she was nearing sixty, Dix could not resist the call to action. Many women around her felt the same way. "I think my duty lies near military hospitals for the present," she wrote to Anne Heath. "This need not be announced, [but] I have reported myself and some nurses for free service at the War Department and to the Surgeon General—".[7]

Thanks to her long-standing connections as a lobbyist in Washington, Dix assumed a position as the first supervisor of women nurses in the United States Army in 1861. She worked in conjunction with the United States Sanitary Commission. The Sanitary Commission was a charitable organization formed in April 1861 and headed by Reverend Henry Bellows and New York architect Frederick Law Olmstead. The organization worked to ensure that Union soldiers were living in clean conditions and had nutritious food to eat. The group had no legal authority, but the strapped Union Army welcomed its involvement.

During her European travels, Dix had heard about Florence Nightingale's nursing work during the Crimean War, fought between Russia and Turkey over control of routes into the Mediterranean Sea, which occurred between 1854 and 1856. Dix decided to emulate Nightingale. A British woman, Nightingale voluntarily went to the war front after Great Britain became involved in the conflict. There, she nursed the soldiers, many of whom were starving, and reformed the military hospitals. When Dix traveled to Turkey in 1856, she took a tour of the hospital, called the Scutari Hospital, where Nightingale had done her work. Nightingale held the semiofficial title of superintendent of the Female Nursing Establishment. She worked largely outside the army structure, much the same way Dix would operate during the Civil War.

Dix's orders originally said that she would work for the army, organizing the hospitals in an official capacity:

> The free services of Miss D. L. Dix are accepted by the War Department, and that she will give at all times all necessary aid in organizing military hospitals for the care of all sick or wounded soldiers, aiding the chief surgeon by supplying nurses and substantial means for the comfort and relief of the suffering; also that she is fully authorized to receive, control, and disburse special supplies bestowed by individuals or associations for the comfort of their friends or the citizen soldiers from all parts of the United States; as also, under sanction of the Acting Surgeon-General, to draw from the army stores.[8]

Her commission also permitted her to recruit women nurses when and if she determined that there was a shortage of male nurses. At the time, women were not allowed to be nurses in hospitals, although many women nursed sick family members as part of their household duties. In the early days of the Civil

War, many of the male nurses were wounded and recovering soldiers. Dix immediately saw the need to recruit women to add to their ranks. Two months after receiving her original commission, she became superintendent of women nurses and set about devising a recruiting and training strategy.

The Medical Department of the Army had strongly resisted the notion of women nurses working in army hospitals. Women were perceived as weak and unable to perform the strenuous duties hospital work might require. Additionally, most men would have been horrified by the thought of being cared for, and seen as vulnerable, by a woman they did not know. The argument against women nurses was threefold: Men argued, "Women are not needed in these hospitals"; said that "ladies are a bore here"; and claimed that the men would be "victimized" by the sheer presence of women.[9] To combat these perceptions, Dix took a practical approach to her task. In order to legitimize the women nurses' position at the front, she compiled an exacting list of qualifications. A woman nurse must be no younger than thirty-five and no older than fifty; in strong health; matronly; of good conduct or superior education with habits of neatness, order, sobriety and industry. A potential nurse must obtain certificates of good character from at least two persons of trust. Dress must be plain—acceptable colors were brown, gray, or black, without ornaments of any sort. A nurse must maintain obedience to rules, and perform all of these requirements for forty cents a day plus subsistence.[10]

Dix took her task very seriously. She often inspected the potential nurses herself and issued them the appropriate papers. One of her charges was Louisa May Alcott, the future author of *Little Women*. Dix sent Alcott, who met the qualifications almost perfectly, to Washington, D.C., to nurse the wounded in 1862. Participation in the war would change Alcott's life. Her experiences led her to write her first published book, *Hospital Sketches*. The book propelled her into the public eye and a lifelong writing career.

Hospital Sketches, a thinly veiled account of Alcott's experience as a nurse, reflected a common theme among the female nurses. Alcott joined the war effort because she wanted "something to do"—much the same reason Dix had become involved in her work for the mentally ill years before.[11]

Dix took her task seriously and did whatever she felt was needed to make sure that the men were receiving the appropriate medical care. The doctors, however, expected the nurses to "do their bidding and never to question the scientific

Louisa May Alcott (seen here), who went on to become a famous children's author, was one of the nurses who served under Dix.

Louisa May Alcott

The author of *Little Women* and more than two hundred other works of fiction was a typical young woman eager to care for the Civil War soldiers. Alcott was thirty years old when she became a nurse in the Georgetown neighborhood of Washington, D.C. The "hospital" where she worked was really the Union Hotel, which had been converted to a hospital. There, she bathed the soldiers, fed them, and wrote letters home for them. Occasionally, she assisted the doctors in the operating room. Because antibiotics had not yet been discovered, the surgeons' most frequent course of action was to amputate the wounded arms or legs of soldiers who had been shot to prevent the wounds from becoming infected.

Alcott's experience was common. She spent long hours tending to the sick, and her exposure to the unsanitary conditions of the hospital caused her to develop typhoid fever. She had spent only six weeks nursing before her father came to take her home to Boston, where it took her months to recover. Alcott was lucky. The hospital's head nurse, Hannah Ropes, died from the same fever.

efficacy of diet or treatment."[12] As a result of her years of philanthropy, Dix's connections were broad and deep. When Surgeon General Robert Wood requested that she find linen for bandages and shirts, Dix called on the women of Boston and reportedly had the supplies the next day.

Butting Heads With the Army

But while Dix persisted in her desire to be in the middle of the action, she refused to work within any organized structure. She had always volunteered her services and been willing to work with the government—but outside its parameters—in order to make changes. Over the years, she found it was an effective way to accomplish her goals of reform. Women could not even vote. Instead, Dix became an expert at the legislative process and an effective lobbyist. As an outsider, she was not as constricted by political organization as some male reformers. But the United States Army demanded rigid structure. Dix soon found that her goals did not mesh with regimented army principles. As the army tried to centralize the power of the Sanitary Commission, Dix encouraged private groups to form their own aid societies.

In the fall of 1861—early in the war—Dix and United States Sanitary Commissioner Reverend Henry Bellows clashed over what he felt was an attempt on her part to organize a Western Sanitary Commission outside the formal structure of the United States Sanitary Commission. Dix had, in fact, traveled to Missouri to establish the group, but her involvement in it was only superficial. Despite this fact, Bellows never quite trusted her again. While she was well respected as a philanthropist, her work remained mostly outside the main Union war efforts.

The Civil War has been called the war "in the housewife's front yard," and Washington, D.C., was

Dix worked with the Sanitary Commission at F Street in Washington, D.C. Often, the predominantly male leadership of the organization clashed with Dix over the proper ways to provide aid to the Union Army.

the front line.[13] It was a virtual Union island surrounded by Confederate Virginia, just over the Potomac River, and Maryland, which was technically part of the Union but contained hundreds of Confederate sympathizers. Several major battles were fought only fifty miles away from Washington, D.C. Those wounded soldiers who were deemed fit enough to travel were brought to Washington to be nursed back to health. As a result, the city was transformed into one large hospital. Churches, Georgetown University, various hotels and federal buildings, even the Capitol (including the House and Senate chambers) were converted to hospitals to care for the wounded.

When Dix took her position with the army, there were no military hospitals in existence. Her organizational skills were in great demand. Acting United States Surgeon General Robert Wood told her, "We are deficient in lint and bandages. I would most respectfully suggest that you institute preliminary measures for these important items of surgical necessity."[14]

Hospitals during the Civil War were often moving units, traveling with the army from battlefield to battlefield.

Throughout her tenure as superintendent of women nurses, Dix recruited more than thirty-two hundred women.[15] One nurse wrote to her, "I am in possession of one of your circulars, and will comply with all your requirements. I am plain-looking enough to suit you, and old enough. I have no near relatives in the war. . . . I never had a husband and am not looking for one—will you take me?"[16]

This recruit was eager to become a nurse and had no fear of Dix's strict demands. To most of the women nurses she recruited, Dix was someone to fear. Although she often took a personal interest in them, her exacting specifications made them refer to her as "dragon Dix" and "a self-sealing can of horror tied up with red tape."[17]

Sometimes, however, Dix could be unexpectedly compassionate. One nurse, Sophronia Bucklin, told the story of how she fell asleep during her watch, only to awaken to find "a tall woman, habited in black" standing before her. The very next day, Bucklin was summoned by Dix. Instead of firing Bucklin for shirking her duty, Dix gave her "a little present" of five dollars—nearly two weeks' pay.[18] And when Louisa May Alcott became ill, Dix herself made sure she received proper care.

In many ways, fifty-nine-year-old Dix was having the time of her life. She wrote to Anne Heath from Washington, "My life is so filled with crowding cares that I do not recollect what time passes between letters received or sent to my friends. . . . I never had so few moments for myself."[19] Although her lobbying efforts had required her to work behind the scenes, her role as the country's head female nurse thrust Dix right into the action. After nearly twenty years of inspecting hospitals, she was now in a position to create field hospitals to care for the wounded.

Unfortunately, the doctors—all of whom were male—resented Dix and her interference. They complained several times to the surgeon general and even to President Lincoln that they did not want Dix arriving unexpectedly to question their authority. On her surprise rounds, Dix occasionally found doctors and hospital stewards (who were in charge of supplies) drunk on duty. Since she felt it was her mission to ensure that the patients were receiving proper care, nothing infuriated her more. After inspecting a hospital one afternoon, much to the chagrin of the steward, Dix made several suggestions for improving the soldiers' care. Frustrated, the steward said, "Madam, who are you that you thus presume to invade my domain and thus dictate to me, the officer in charge?" Dix reportedly looked the man directly in the eye and said, "I am Dorothea L. Dix, Superintendent of Nurses, in the employ of the United States Government." After she left, the man asked another officer who Dix was. The officer said, "Why man alive, don't you know her? Why, she has the rank . . . honors, and emoluments of a major-general of volunteers and if you have got her down on you, you might as well have all hell after you."[20]

The Final Battle

Dix's power, however, did not last. Many complaints were lodged, and in October 1863, the assistant surgeon general issued General Order 351. It said that Dix could continue to issue "certificates of approval" for her women nurse recruits, but that the male surgeons would have the sole authority to give final approval. Moreover, once they were hired, women nurses would report to a hospital's medical director.

Dix was deeply hurt. After serving the war effort tirelessly for over two years, her power had been taken away. Despite this fact, she stubbornly refused to resign her post. She kept her formal title until 1866.

Although she grew to view her Civil War experience as a mere footnote in her own life, Dix is often better known for that brief interlude than for her many years of work on behalf of the mentally ill. After carefully avoiding the political and social issues of slavery and even women's rights, the war put Dix square in the middle of them. Without trying, she empowered women by providing them with important, life-changing work. And while she consistently sidestepped the slavery issue, through nursing she was working to preserve the Union, a move that would ultimately lead to the freeing of the Southern slaves.

War Memorial

When the war ended after Confederate General Robert E. Lee surrendered to Union General Ulysses Grant at Appomattox Court House, Virginia, in April 1865, Dix set about erecting a war monument to the soldiers who had died in battle. Soliciting private donations from friends, she raised enough money for a memorial by the middle of 1866. Eventually, Dix sought the support of President Ulysses Grant and Secretary of War Edwin Stanton for her plan. Her memorial was erected in a cemetery at Fortress Monroe in Hampton, Virginia, where thousands of Civil War soldiers were laid to rest. When Stanton asked her how she wished to be honored for her own service in the war effort, she simply said she wanted "the flag of my country." To her surprise, he sent her a flag in December 1868. "No greater distinction could have been conferred upon me," Dix wrote in return. She added, "No possession will be so prized while life remains to love and serve my country."[21]

On the Road Again

Her war work completed, Dix took to the road once again, traveling throughout the country inspecting her hospitals for the mentally ill. By this time, she was well into her sixties. Despite pleas from her friends, she still refused to slow down.

After a brief visit to her good friend Anne Heath, Dix began a tour of all the hospitals she had worked to establish. She also struck out into new territory, going as far south as Florida and as far west as California, where she actually found that her services were unneeded—the state was already providing good care for the mentally ill.

Everywhere she went, Dix was met with the success and appreciation that had eluded her during the

Soldiers' Home in Washington, D.C., would become the Army Veteran Hospital founded by Dorothea Dix.

Civil War. The Pennsylvania legislature voted to expand its second hospital for the mentally ill and provided money for a third hospital to be built. Dix also convinced the Connecticut legislature to establish a hospital there. She traveled back to Washington, D.C., to appeal for additional money for St. Elizabeth's Hospital. The war had wounded many soldiers and the hospital was in need of expansion.

Dix made her way through the South as well. She found that the war had truly devastated the region.

There were scarce resources for the mentally ill. Dix was welcomed in the South like a hero returning from war. In Raleigh, North Carolina, the governor himself accompanied her into the state capitol. There, she was given an honorary seat on the Senate floor and the senators "rose in silent tribute."[22]

The postwar era, referred to as Reconstruction because it was a time of rebuilding the nation, was harsh for Dix's hospitals in North and South Carolina in particular. The lack of staff and money to repair damaged buildings meant that many of the hospital patients were once again locked into rooms or, worse, even restrained with chains or straitjackets. The doctors were simply overwhelmed. "It would seem, that all my work is to be done over so far as the insane are concerned," Dix wrote to a friend. "Language is too poor to describe the miserable state of these poor wretches in dungeon cells."[23]

But nearing the age of seventy, Dix would not have the strength to continue her work. While traveling in Kentucky in 1870, she became ill with a cough. In a short time, Dix returned to the New Jersey State Lunatic Asylum in Trenton, the hospital she called her "first born." Through her friendship with the hospital superintendent, Horace Buttolph, the asylum was becoming the closest thing to a home for Dix.

Doctors there diagnosed her with malaria, a disease transmitted by mosquitoes that causes chills and fever. She had probably caught the illness in the swampy landscape of Washington during her Civil War nursing years. Although some doctors felt Dix would not survive, she recovered, and amazingly, began to travel yet again. She wrote to Anne Heath from Washington, D.C., "Now if you think I am idle any part of the working time for the twenty-four hours, you are mistaken. I have all the time and have always as much as I can do."[24]

Honoring "Our Lady"

By 1877, the nationally known Dix was described as a "little old woman in her dark dress, shawl and bonnet, who wore a bit of red, white, and blue ribbon upon her breast as proudly as any soldier wore his army button."[25] It was time for her to be honored for her lifetime of service. She had founded thirty-two state-run mental hospitals and one federal hospital, St. Elizabeth's in Washington, D.C. Her work had brought so much attention to the plight of the mentally ill that 123 hospitals had been established by 1880, 75 of which were operated by the states. When Dixmont Hospital unveiled a portrait of Dix, the superintendent, John Harper, referred to her in exalted terms as if she were a saint: "The mission of 'our Lady' is to create those noble institutions which aid in the restoration of the dethroned reason, and Dixmont Hospital is one of the jewels which will adorn her crown thereafter."[26] Another portrait of Dix was placed in the chapel of St. Elizabeth's Hospital. Soon, six other hospitals she had founded placed her portrait in a place of honor.

Although she continued to travel, she did so at a less frantic pace. The news of her brother Joseph's death, followed closely by Anne Heath's death in 1878, saddened her greatly. She was forced to think about her own mortality. In her will, Dix instructed her executor to invest her money until it grew to $50,000, then put it toward the civic education of America's youth.[27]

In 1876, Dix's good friend Horace Buttolph helped establish a permanent residence for her at the New Jersey State Hospital in Trenton. While living there, she received famous visitors such as Hack Tuke, the grandson of William Tuke, founder of England's York Retreat, on which she based the compassionate care concept for her hospitals.

Dix remained in Trenton until she died on July 17, 1887. She was buried in the Mount Auburn Cemetery. Her simple headstone contained only her name, "Dorothea L. Dix."

8

DIX'S LEGACY

Today, Dorothea Dix is remembered as a great reformer. She is often referred to as a "crusader" for the mentally ill. She relentlessly pursued her objective—to provide adequate care for the poor mentally ill in the United States and abroad. But the way she accomplished her goal is both unique and memorable. Instead of working only through private individuals or charitable organizations like most reformers of her time, Dix worked within the halls of government as an individual intent on establishing a system of standard public treatment for the mentally ill.

Dix went directly to the halls of government to lobby and convince state and federal lawmakers that the care of the mentally ill should not be left to charitable organizations alone. It should be the responsibility of the government.

Her tireless efforts, her continuous focus, and her power to persuade lawmakers made her the nation's most influential female lobbyist of the day. It could be argued that she was the most influential lobbyist— male or female—of her time as she traveled to the states, working to establish hospitals.

While Dix established or helped to establish nearly 128 hospitals, her success is particularly extraordinary because she was a woman. At the time, she could not even cast a vote for the legislators she was trying so hard to persuade. Women today can make countless choices about how they want to live their lives, but in the 1800s, it was unusual for a woman to remain single and to be so focused on her career.

Dix is remarkable not only in that she accomplished her goals of raising money from private donors and convincing state legislators to fund the construction and operation of hospitals, but also because she transformed the type of care received by mentally ill patients. No longer would people who suffered from mental illnesses such as schizophrenia or depression be kept locked away in chains, hidden in shame from society's view. Dix argued successfully that the mentally ill should receive medical treatment. She was among the first to destigmatize mental illness.

In the early to mid-1800s, America as a nation was debating how involved the government should be in people's lives, both at the state and federal levels—a debate that continues even today. It was Dix who stood up, spoke, and ultimately persuaded lawmakers that the country's poorest and most helpless inhabitants, the indigent mentally ill, should be cared for by the government. No one had yet done this so convincingly or so thoroughly. By speaking out and by being persistent, Dix helped weave the social fabric of the nation by providing state-run services that we often take for granted today.

CHRONOLOGY

1802—*April 2*: Born in Hampden, Maine (part of Massachusetts at the time).

1809—Grandfather Dix dies.

1814—Goes to Boston to live with Grandmother Dix.

1816—Moves to Worcester, Massachusetts, to live with her great aunt Sarah Fiske; Opens a dame school in Worcester.

1819—Returns to Boston to live with Grandmother Dix.

1821—Opens a school in grandmother's mansion, Orange Court; Also opens a charitable school for poor children; Father, Joseph Dix, dies.

1824—Publishes *Conversations on Common Things*.

1826—Health fails due to lung problems and exhaustion; Closes her schools.

1827—Writes four more books.
–1829

1830—Travels to Virgin Islands with minister William Ellery Channing and his family.

1831—Reopens schools in Boston.

1836—Health fails again; Closes her schools.

1836—Travels to England and recovers health at
–1837 Greenbank, an estate near Liverpool, England, owned by the Rathbone family; Grandmother Dix dies; Mother, Mary Bigelow Dix, dies.

1839—Brother Charles Wesley lost at sea and presumed dead.

1841—*March 28*: Views for the first time the poor treatment received by mentally ill prisoners in the East Cambridge, Massachusetts, jail.

1842—Conducts a statewide tour of prisons and almshouses where mentally ill are kept.

1843—*January*: Presents a moving memorial to the Massachusetts legislature; Begins investigating mental institutions in Nova Scotia and New York.

1844—Tours Rhode Island facilities for the mentally ill.

1845—Addresses the legislatures of New Jersey and Pennsylvania.

1845 –1846—Begins touring facilities for the mentally ill in Tennessee, Kentucky, Ohio, and Maryland.

1846 –1847—Travels to the Deep South; Tours Louisiana, Alabama, Georgia, South Carolina, Mississippi, and Arkansas.

1848—*June 23*: Her legislation requesting 5 million acres of public lands be set aside for the care of the mentally ill is introduced in Congress.

1849—Travels to Alabama, Mississippi, Louisiana, Illinois, Ohio, and North Carolina to campaign for better care for the mentally ill.

1850—Land grant bill passed by House of Representatives; Senate fails to consider the bill.

1851—Land grant bill passed by United States Senate; House fails to vote on it.

1852—President Fillmore signs an executive order authorizing the construction of Army and Navy Hospital (now known as St. Elizabeth's) in Washington, D.C.

1853—Visits Sable Island.

1854—Land grant bill passed by both House and Senate but vetoed by President Franklin Pierce.

1855—Takes her crusade to Scotland and the Channel Islands.

1856—Tours Italy and meets with Pope Pius IX, asking him to improve the treatment of mentally ill people in Rome; Visits Greece, Turkey, Austria-Hungary, Germany, Russia, and Scandinavia; Returns to America.

1858—Travels to Texas and elsewhere in the South.
–1859

1861—Appointed as superintendent of women nurses of the United States Army; Serves in this capacity until 1866.

1862—Personally recruits Louisa May Alcott to nurse in Washington, D.C.

1867—Raises funds for soldiers' monument.

1869—Travels to California.

1878—Friend Anne Heath dies; Brother Joseph dies.

1881—*October 1*: Begins touring the South one last time; Arrives at Trenton hospital in New Jersey exhausted and ill.

1887—*July 17*: Dies in her apartment at Trenton hospital, New Jersey.

CHAPTER NOTES

Chapter 1. "I Tell What I Have Seen"

1. Dorothea L. Dix, "Memorial to the Legislature of Massachusetts," *On Behalf of the Insane Poor Selected Reports* (New York: Arno Press, 1971), p. 4.

2. Ibid., pp. 3–4.

3. Ibid., p. 3.

4. Ibid., p. 6.

5. Ibid., p. 10.

6. Ibid., p. 7.

7. Ibid., p. 31.

8. Ibid., p. 32.

Chapter 2. Out of the Wilderness

1. David Gollaher, *Voice for the Mad: The Life of Dorothea Dix* (New York: Free Press, 1995), p. 9.

2. Helen Marshall, *Dorothea Dix, Forgotten Samaritan* (Chapel Hill: University of North Carolina Press, 1937), p. 5.

3. Francis Tiffany, *The Life of Dorothea L. Dix* (Ann Arbor, Mich.: Plutarch Press, 1971), p. 8.

4. Gollaher, p. 17.

5. Tiffany, p. 11.

Chapter 3. Learning to Be a Lady

1. Helen Marshall, *Dorothea Dix, Forgotten Samaritan* (Chapel Hill: University of North Carolina Press, 1937), p. 14.

2. Francis Tiffany, *The Life of Dorothea L. Dix* (Ann Arbor, Mich.: Plutarch Press, 1971), p. 9.

3. Marshall, p. 18.

4. Alfred S. Roe, *Dorothea Lynde Dix*, A paper read before the Worcester Society of Antiquity, November 20, 1888 (Worcester, Mass.: Franklin P. Rice, 1889), p. 9.

5. Marshall, p. 22.

6. Ibid., p. 24.

7. Ibid., p. 33.

8. David Gollaher, *Voice for the Mad: The Life of Dorothea Dix* (New York: Free Press, 1995), p. 35.

9. Ibid.

10. Ibid., p. 36.

11. Marshall, p. 36.

Chapter 4. Journeys Outward

1. David Gollaher, *Voice for the Mad: The Life of Dorothea Dix* (New York: Free Press, 1995), p. 52.

2. Ibid., p. 69.

3. Ibid., p. 74.

4. Ibid., p. 110.

5. Francis Tiffany, *The Life of Dorothea L. Dix* (Ann Arbor, Mich.: Plutarch Press, 1971), p. 51.

6. Gollaher, p. 120.

Chapter 5. Starting Her Life's Work

1. B. O. Flowers, "Treatment of the Insane Poor in Massachusetts Sixty Years Ago; or How a Woman Wrought a Revolution in Human Progress," *Arena*, XXXII (1904), pp. 535–542.

2. David Gollaher, *Voice for the Mad: The Life of Dorothea Dix* (New York: Free Press, 1995), p. 159.

3. Ibid., p. 155.

4. Ibid., p. 166.

5. Ibid., p. 164.

6. Francis Tiffany, *The Life of Dorothea L. Dix* (Ann Arbor, Mich.: Plutarch Press, 1971), pp. 130–131.

7. Helen Marshall, *Dorothea Dix, Forgotten Samaritan* (Chapel Hill: University of North Carolina Press, 1937), p. 99.

8. Ibid., p. 101.

9. Ibid., p. 100.

10. Ibid.

11. F. B. Sanborn, *Memoirs of Pliny Earle, M.D.* (Boston: Damrell & Upham, 1898), pp. 307–308.

12. Marshall, p. 102.

13. Dorothea Dix, *Memorial Soliciting a State Hospital for the Insane* (Trenton: n.p., January 23, 1845), p. 3.

14. Frederick Herrmann, *Dorothea L. Dix and the Politics of Institutional Reform* (Trenton: New Jersey Historical Commission, 1981), p. 25.

15. Gollaher, pp. 193–194.

16. Ibid., p. 193.

17. Herrmann, p. 28.

18. Ibid., p. 29.

19. Gollaher, p. 205.

20. Ibid.

21. Tiffany, p. 132.

22. Ibid.

23. Ibid., p. 146.

Chapter 6. To the Capitol!

1. Francis Tiffany, *The Life of Dorothea L. Dix* (Ann Arbor, Mich.: Plutarch Press, 1971), p. 134.

2. Helen Marshall, *Dorothea Dix, Forgotten Samaritan* (Chapel Hill: University of North Carolina Press, 1937), pp. 129–130.

3. Frederick Herrmann, *Dorothea Dix and the Politics of Institutional Reform* (Trenton: New Jersey Historical Commission, 1981), p. 31.

4. David Gollaher, *Voice for the Mad: The Life of Dorothea Dix* (New York: Free Press, 1995), p. 282.

5. Dorothea L. Dix, *On Behalf of the Insane Poor Selected Reports* (New York: Arno Press, 1971), p. 5.

6. Ibid., pp. 8, 9.

7. Ibid., p. 32.

8. Gollaher, p. 287.

9. Ibid., p. 289.

10. Ibid., p. 300.

11. Ibid., p. 302.

12. Ibid., p. 305.

13. Ibid., p. 312.

14. Marshall, p. 148.

15. Ibid., p. 151.

16. Gollaher, p. 330.

17. Ibid., p. 337.

18. Ibid., p. 342.

19. Marshall, p. 175.

20. Ibid., p. 176.

Chapter 7. Back Home, Back to War

1. David Gollaher, *Voice for the Mad: The Life of Dorothea Dix* (New York: Free Press, 1995), pp. 383–385.

2. Ibid., p. 387.

3. Ibid., p. 389.

4. Francis Tiffany, *The Life of Dorothea L. Dix* (Ann Arbor, Mich.: Plutarch Press, 1971), p. 331.

5. Ibid., p. 334.

6. Ibid.

7. Ibid., p. 336.

8. *The War of the Rebellion, A Compilation of the Official Records of the Union and Confederate Armies* (Washington, D.C.: U.S. Government Printing Office), series III, vol. 2, p. 107.

9. *Notes of Hospital Life from November 1861 to August 1863* (Philadelphia: J. B. Lippincott, 1864), p. 18.

10. Bessie Jones, "Introduction," in Louisa May Alcott, *Hospital Sketches*, ed. Bessie Jones (Cambridge: Belknap Press, 1960), p. xxviii.

11. Louisa May Alcott, *Hospital Sketches*, ed. Bessie Jones (Cambridge: Belknap Press, 1960), p. 7.

12. Jane Schultz, *Women at the Front: Gender and Genre in Literature of the American Civil War*, Ph.D. Dissertation, 1988, p. 74.

13. Jones, p. xvii.

14. Helen Marshall, *Dorothea Dix, Forgotten Samaritan* (Chapel Hill: University of North Carolina Press, 1937), p. 204.

15. Schultz, p. 69.

16. Jones, p. xxxviii.

17. Cornelia Hancock, *South After Gettysburg: Letters of Cornelia Hancock, 1863–1868*, ed. Henrietta Stratton Jaquette (New York: Crowell, 1956), p. 131.

18. Sophronia Bucklin, *In Hospital and Camp* (Philadelphia: John E. Potter & Co., 1869), pp. 60–61.

19. Marshall, p. 211.

20. Ibid., p. 220.

21. Ibid., p. 231.

22. Gollaher, p. 432.

23. Marshall, p. 239.

24. Ibid., p. 240.

25. Ibid.

26. Tiffany, pp. 354–355.

27. Gollaher, p. 445.

GLOSSARY

almshouse—A place maintained at public expense to house poor people with nowhere else to stay.

apothecary—A pharmacy or drugstore where medicines are made or dispensed.

destigmatize—To take away the notion of shame or disgrace.

executor—The person appointed to carry out a will.

focal point—A center of activity, attraction, or attention.

idiot—An old-fashioned term for a person with a diminished mental capacity who requires complete care.

imagery—Mental pictures, especially the products of imagination.

indigent—A poor person who has no home or a job.

insanity—A deranged state of the mind, usually occurring as a specific disorder.

lunacy—Insanity amounting to a lack of mental capacity or responsibility in the eyes of the law.

mental illness—An illness of the mind, such as depression or schizophrenia.

opulent—Rich or lavish.

Parliament—A supreme legislative body in certain nations.

philanthropists—People who engage in acts of charity or goodwill.

philanthropy—Charity; the active effort to promote human welfare.

secession—Formal withdrawal from an organization or country.

state sovereignty—State freedom from the control of the federal government.

FURTHER READING

Colman, Penny. *Breaking the Chains: The Crusade of Dorothea Lynde Dix.* White Hall, Va.: Shoe Tree Press, 1992.

Malone, Mary. *Dorothea L. Dix: Hospital Founder.* New York: Chelsea Juniors, 1991.

Schlaifer, Charles. *Heart's Work: Civil War Heroine and Champion of the Mentally Ill.* New York: Paragon House, 1991.

Schleichert, Elizabeth. *The Life of Dorothea Dix.* Frederick, Md.: Twenty-First Century Books, 1992.

Warrick, Karen Clemens. *Louisa May Alcott: Author of Little Women.* Berkeley Heights, N. J.: Enslow Publishers, Inc., 2000.

INTERNET ADDRESSES

Agriculture and Education in Colonial America. January 5, 1999. <http://www.cals.ncsu.edu/agexed/aee501/show1/sld001.htm>.

"Dorothea Dix." *The Home of The American Civil War.* n.d. <http://www.civilwarhome.com/dixbio.htm>.

Encyclopedia Britannica. "Dix, Dorothea Lynde." *Women in American History.* 1999. <http://women.eb.com/women/articles/Dix_Dorothea_Lynde.html>.

National Alliance for the Mentally Ill. *NAMI: The Nation's Voice on Mental Illness.* 1996–2001. <http://www.nami.org/>.

United States Sanitary Commission. "The Beginnings." *United States Sanitary Commission.* 1997–2000. <http://www.netwalk.com/~jpr/History1.htm>.

INDEX